ROBERT K. HUDNUT is pastor of St. Luke Presbyterian Church in suburban Minneapolis and President of the Greater Metropolitan Federation of Minneapolis. He is the author of SURPRISED BY GOD, A SENSITIVE MAN AND THE CHRIST, and A THINKING MAN AND THE CHRIST.

THE SLEEPING GIANT

ROBERT K. HUDNUT

THE SLEEPING GIANT

Arousing Church Power in America

HARPER & ROW, PUBLISHERS

New York, Evanston, San Francisco, London

75% say religion is losing its influence on American life.
Gallup Poll, 1970

I fear the silence of the churches more
than the shouts of the angry multitudes.
—MARTIN LUTHER KING, JR.

These men who have turned the world upside down . . .
—ACTS 17:6

*To the beautiful people
who are St. Luke Presbyterian Church,
Wayzata, Minnesota*

Contents

Preface

This book is for the person who belongs to a church but has the feeling his church is not quite making it in the 1970's.

It is for the man or woman who is a member of one of the most powerful organizations in the world, yet sees that organization continually frustrated in the release of its power.

It is for the man or woman who wants to make his church at the corner of State and Main *work*.

It is *not* for people who think the local church, all things considered, is doing a pretty good job.

It is *not* for people in churches who want to keep things as they are.

It *is* for people who think they can, with discipline and honor, recover some of the toughness and verve of the first-century church.

The author is pastor of a Presbyterian church in suburban Minneapolis.

1

A Church that Means Business
or
No Discipline—No Disciples

I

In many quarters a dangerous euphoria envelops the American church. For years the church in America has been mesmerized by its "success." It has been infatuated with its buildings, budgets, and bromides. It has nurtured the illusion that it is relevant, that it is saying something, that it is reaching people where they live.

It is high time we chucked such genial fictions. The church in many quarters is in trouble, and the sooner we realize it the better. When nearly two-thirds of your membership do not show up for your weekly meeting, your organization is in trouble.[1] When your members give no more per week to alleviating world suffering—a goal for which their founder was famous—than the price of a hot dog at a ball park, your organization is in trouble.[2] When it takes the combined efforts of ten thousand of your members to win three new members a year, then you are very close to being on the rocks.[3] And when your organization has little to say about the great social issues of the day—from Black Power to Vietnam—it *is* on the rocks.

No longer can we afford to treat the church as the sanctifier of the status quo. No longer can we tolerate its simpering irrelevance. It is time to *refuse* membership to any who are not dead serious about the claims that membership makes upon them.

And it is time to *erase* from membership those who treat their membership cavalierly.

Most churches could be two-thirds smaller and lose nothing in power. Few pastors would dare to say that more than one-third of their church are really responding to the claims of Christ. The second third are peripheral. And the third third are out. The pastors themselves are often as blissfully supine as their people.

The church is a club. It is a cadre. It is a highly *ex*clusive organization. It has the most stringent standards of membership of any organization in the world. "If any man would come after me," its founder said, "let him deny himself and take up his cross and follow me." If we can't buy the standards, then we should stay out of the church. If we're in and not measuring up, then we should either measure up or get out.

Too long have American churches seduced people for Christ. Lest the language be thought unduly harsh, it should be remembered that Webster's first definition of "seduce" is "to persuade (one) as into disobedience, disloyalty, or desertion of a lord or a cause." The soft sell of a soft gospel has attracted soft people to soft jobs, but it has not "turned the world upside down" for Jesus Christ. It has not "made disciples of all nations." It has not driven wealthy American churchmen into the ghettos, slums, and gutters of the world to pick up the children who are segregated, improverished, and starved.

So the church is finding that it is full of perjurers. We have stood up in front of hundreds of witnesses and have said that we "confess Jesus Christ as our Lord and Savior." But there are people in churches who never crack the Bible, never pray with each other, never do anything for racial justice. Half the world goes to bed hungry, according to the UN; and the church's response is a few boxcars of powdered milk at Easter. Two-thirds of the world is not Christian; and the church's response is a nickel per member per week to foreign missions.

The standards of a Boy Scout troop are higher than those of the Christian church. If you miss four times at a service club, you're out. If you fail to show up for work, you're fired.

It is high time the church got tough. Christ preached a tough gospel in tough times for tough men. And it takes an iron will to measure up. If we can't measure up, then let's stay out of the church. If we're in and not measuring up, then let's either measure up or get out.

As the late Halford Luccock put it in his commentary on the rich man who turned away sorrowing from Christ,

Jesus did not tone down his message for the sake of winning a desirable disciple; He set it forth in all its stern fullness. He never offered bargains; He never concealed the cross, or disguised the cost. That is the only way in which real disciples are ever won. . . . Christ "lost his man," but He did not lose His gospel.[4]

II

Certainly one way to recover the gospel is to recover one of its cutting edges. This particular edge is the one the great German pastor Bonhoeffer tried so valiantly to recover. It cost him his life, and in no small part for that reason it is an edge that cuts today. It is the cutting edge of obedience.

"Your obedience," we are reminded in the last chapter of Romans, "is known to all." "He was obedient," wrote Paul of Christ, "even to death."

Unless he obeys [Bonhoeffer wrote], a man cannot believe. The step of obedience must be taken *before* faith can be possible. . . . If you dismiss the word of God's command, you will not receive His word of grace. . . . The gracious call of Jesus now becomes a stern command: Do this! Give up that! Leave the ship and come to me! . . . Jesus says: *First* obey, perform the *external* work. . . . If you don't believe, take the first step all the same, for you are bidden to take it. No one wants to know about your faith or unbelief, your *orders* are to perform the act of obedience on the spot. *Then* you will find yourself in the situation where faith becomes possible.[5]

Many years ago, in some cases centuries ago, we tried to get obedience back. We wrote membership vows or their equivalent in a valiant effort to keep this cutting edge of the gospel, to spell our obedience out.

Unfortunately, however, such constitutional measures, although excellent, have been honored more in the breach than in the observance. The national Protestant attendance average is 37 percent, which means that nearly two-thirds of the membership are somewhere else on Sunday morning. The national Protestant giving average is $87.00,[6] which works out to two dimes and four pennies a day. Seventy-five percent, according to the latest Gallup Poll, say that religion is losing its influence on American life.

In the face of this appalling statistical evidence, it is belaboring the obvious to say that church members dishonor their vows. What is perhaps more helpful is to suggest that at last the time has come to beef those vows up. First we had the vows to spell out the commands of Christ. Now we need a discipline to spell out the vows. If a person does not want to be obedient to that discipline then I would respectfully suggest that there is no point whatever in his belonging to a Christian church. No discipline—no disciple.

"Life," said Robert Frost, "is tons of discipline." And he could not have been more correct for church people. At best they have only a fragile conception that anything is *required* of them as church members. At worst they are merely along for the ride.

The fact of the matter is that a basic Christian discipline, in three equal parts, going all the way back to the first century, *is* required of *all* church members. If they don't like the discipline then they had better not join the church, just as if they don't like the discipline of reporting for work, they had better not join the firm.

Now I hold no brief for this discipline's being the best or the only discipline. It is simply a discipline that evolved for one person as he worked his way through the New Testament trying to find some solution to the problem of the irrelevant church. Over the last few years we have used these disciplines at our church and seen the percentage evidence and other evidence of commitment build.

III

A *first* requirement of the church member is that he study. "They devoted themselves," we read in the book of Acts (2:42), "to the apostles' teaching." "Great are the works of the Lord," wrote a psalmist, "studied by all who have pleasure in them" (Ps. 111:2).

A disciple is a "learner" in the root sense of the word. It is impossible to obey Christ's commands, or any of the other commands in the Bible for that matter, without knowing exactly what was said and exactly what was meant. This requires good hard solid work with the mind. The Christian church begins and ends with the Bible, the *kerygma,* the proclamation. But we can't possibly understand the Bible unless we undertake the discipline of studying the Bible, just as we cannot understand business or labor problems unless we study business or labor problems.

Now the only such study that goes on is, in large part, sandwiched into 47 minutes on Sunday morning. Let's not kid ourselves that our children are taught anything in their homes. It just isn't being done, except by filtration, in the vast majority of families. Nor should we kid ourselves that the rest of us are really learning very much in our churches. Beyond a bland little homily on Sunday morning, most of us do not come to intellectual grips with our faith.

Most churches function at a high level of well-intentioned mediocrity, and when it comes to demanding any kind of rigorous thinking through of the implications of one's faith, most churches back off. It is really staggering how little thinking goes on in churches. We leave our brains on our jobs, which is understandable if not commendable. THINK is the motto of one of our great corporations. "Thought out" is the motto of many churches.

Few parents would be so bold as to say they knew more about the Bible than their children. As a matter of fact, a few years ago we had a little Sunday morning quiz in our church service. "Name the first book of the Bible." "Who came first—David or Moses?" Questions like that. The average grade was a stunning 26 percent. "Who were the Pharisees?" "The bad guys in black hats." "What were the Epistles?" "The wives of the apostles."

In other words, the average Protestant (which is no news) is a Biblical illiterate. "The church," writes a Presbyterian commentator, "is destructively, perversely, tragically, malignantly, willfully ignorant."

And yet the church was responsible for the first universities. The church has produced many of the great thinkers of the world. And it was the church that "devoted itself to the apostles' teaching" and then went out with that teaching and "turned the world upside down" (Acts 17:6).

What we have lost in our churches is the thrill of learning. There is no other word for it. Let's get it back by

One. Offering courses—not just classes but courses. Let's go for four weeks in them, for the school term, for a year even. Let's bring in experts, the way we do in our businesses. Let's hire them, each of us putting down $5.00, $10.00, or even $25.00 to *learn* about our religion and how it relates to business, politics, family, Vietnam.

Two. Let's expand our church schools to include our homes. Every parent should go over every church school lesson with his child. If there are five children, then there are five lessons, first with the father, the age-old spiritual leader in the home, and then with the mother. Children should not bring their parents to church unless their parents have first done their homework with them in the home.

Three. Let's get the thrill of learning back into our churches by experimenting. The church is a laboratory. It is a laboratory for basic and applied religious research. Laboratories are exciting. People are looking for breakthroughs in laboratories. They are not afraid to experiment. They are not afraid to fail. We should be willing in our churches to try *anything* that will deepen our discipleship and contribute to the discipleship of others. "Go," Christ said in his great commission to the church, "Go . . . and make disciples of all nations." No discipline—no discipleship.

IV

A *second* requirement of the church member is that he share. The word the early Christians used was *koinonia*. "They devoted themselves to the apostles' teaching and fellowship [*koinonia*]." The word was used two ways. The first is the more familiar. It is the personal form of sharing.

This is the kind of sharing, or fellowship, which the Christian church has made famous. The church is perhaps the one social institution in which deep sharing can take place. Where else can people be so honest? Where else can they relate to each other in such depth? "If one member suffers," Paul wrote, "all suffer together. If one member is honored, all rejoice together" (1 Cor. 12:26). "Bear one another's burdens," he said, "and so fulfill the law of Christ" (Gal. 6:2).

Now there are, or can be, in every church at least two regular opportunities for this kind of deep personal sharing. One is the sharing of the large group. This is what we might call the one great hour of sharing at the beginning of every week on Sunday morning. The beloved community gathers to share what is most on its heart—its love for God, its concern for others, its anxiety about itself.

In a church that means business, every member will be accounted for on Sunday morning. Either he will be at divine worship or he will be sick, or he will be worshiping or ministering elsewhere.

In an access of revolt against Jewish legalism or Roman Catholic works theology, or simply in an access of rationalization to cover indolence, we say that we are not obligated to worship on the first day. This is not true. Just as the employee reports to work on Monday morning, so the Christian employee also reports to work on Sunday morning. If he doesn't like what's going on, then he works to change it.

The one great hour of sharing on Sunday morning is not negotiable. What if only half the team showed up for a game? What if a doctor failed to show up for an operation? What if a mother failed to show up for dinner? What if a businessman, and there are plenty of them in our churches, failed to show up for a management meeting?

If a person does not want to accept the discipline of weekly worship that is his prerogative, but there is no point whatever in his being a member of the Christian church. This means that two-thirds of American Protestants and one-third of American Catholics could resign. The alternative is to participate in Sunday worship. It's a good one.

*

The other form of personal sharing is the small group. Great things are happening in churches these days because of small groups. All the first churches were small groups. All experienced the deep Christian fellowship known as *koinonia* right in their own homes. All did, or tried to do, what Paul taught in his letter to the small group at Galatia: "Bear one another's burdens and so fulfill the law of Christ."

Twenty centuries later we suffer from cathedralitis. We have what is called an edifice complex. We have to have a big building and a big membership and a big budget, or we feel we have failed. Now there is nothing wrong with bigness as such, but there is plenty wrong with it if it prevents the deep Christian fellowship of the first-century church which turned the world upside down.

What we must do is build small groups into our churches. We must structure for love. They will be the church in microcosm, with everyone in the small group being obedient to the three disciplines of church membership.

"Bear one another's burdens." But we can't bear the burdens

of 600 other people. We can bear the burdens of six, perhaps, or eight or twelve. I can help bear the burdens of the few people who can sit in my living room. And they can help me bear mine. The church are those who, incredible as it may seem, bear one another's burdens.

He who is alone with his sin [wrote Bonhoeffer] is utterly alone. It may be that Christians, notwithstanding corporate worship, common prayer, and all their fellowship in service, may still be left to their loneliness. The final breakthrough to fellowship does not occur, because, though they have fellowship with one another as believers and as devout people, they do not have fellowship as the undevout, as sinners.[7]

The church are the community of the shared life. They are the people who will share each other's depths as well as heights. They are those who will bear one another's burdens. If you don't find love, then it isn't the church.

*   *   *

The other form of sharing is what we might call impersonal sharing. Every member of a church that means business will be involved in it. This was the other meaning of the word *koinonia*. It meant the sharing of money.

"If any man would come after me," Christ said, "let him deny himself." A *condition* of church membership is sacrifice. "Sell what you have," he said to the rich man, "and give to the poor." Sacrificial giving to meet the agony of our time is a *condition* of church membership. If we do not want to give sacrificially that is our prerogative. But let us not at the same time festoon our names on the membership role of a local church. After all, Jesus let the rich man go. He could not fulfill a *condition* of church membership, so he did not join the church.

The *only* standard for Christian giving is sacrifice. And one of the best standards for sacrifice I know anything about is the tithe. We affluent Americans should give away at least 10 percent of our incomes. People in higher brackets, and there are plenty of them in our churches, should give even more. The government allows up to 50 percent of adjusted gross income as tax-deductible for charity giving. People in very low brackets should give less. The point is, whatever the percentage of income, it should be sacrificial. And the tithe is unquestionably one of the best indicators of sacrifice there is. "Of all that thou givest me," Jacob said, "I will give the tenth to thee" (Gen. 28:22).

Why is it that the poorer churches tithe and the richer ones tip? What is it about affluence that bewitches us into holding on to our possessions? The Church of the Nazarene and the Church of God are far out in front of their nearest competitors in giving. To be sure, they have fewer members. But that is just the point. No tithe—no join. They are "poor people's" churches. Episcopalians, who are far richer, are 44th in the order of giving—$155 per capita behind the Church of the Nazarene.[8] United Presbyterians are 25th. The United Church of Christ is a dispirited 29th. Those are three of the "highest-class" denominations in America, which means that, as far as church giving goes, the higher the class the lower the giving; the more the affluence the less the generosity; the more the wealth the less the compassion.

The *only* answer to weak church giving is to *require* sacrificial giving as a *condition* of church membership. If you don't want to give sacrificially, then don't join the organization whose founder demanded that people give sacrificially. If you are already a member of his organization, then either give sacrificially or get out. In the name of Christian compassion around the world we can do no less. "I was hungry," Christ said, "and you gave me food" (Matt. 25:35).

V

A *last* requirement of the church member is that he serve. He studies, he shares, and he serves. Note the verbs. This is Old

Testament action theology as well as New. Note also the alliteration, which is of course mnemonically helpful.

Every member of a church that means business is expected to serve because every member is a minister. Everyone participates in what the first church called their *diakonia*. "If anyone serves me," Jesus said, "the Father will honor him" (John 12:26). "Discipleship," a scholar explains, "demands service even to death."[9] Again, no discipline—no disciple.

The word "minister," coming from the Latin, means "one who serves." The word for clergy in the New Testament referred to *all* Christians. The word for laity in the New Testament referred to *all* Christians. We are all ministers. We are all servants of Jesus Christ.

Every Christian has a major and minor ministry. His major ministry is his job and his home. His minor ministry is some one thing at least which he takes on, because of his church membership, to serve other people. "I was sick and you visited me," Christ said, "I was in prison and you came to me" (Matt. 25:36).

Christ himself was the Suffering Servant, and the trouble is now, when we take our membership vows, either because they have become hackneyed or because we are not paying attention, we are unable to imagine the church as a community of suffering servants. *Then* when you confessed Christ it was in the arena. *Then* when you worshiped it was a capital crime. Now, on our enormous incomes by the world's standards, we do not know what it is to suffer. And we are so isolated from the suffering that does go on that the call to serve the hungry and the poor and the sick and imprisoned is often too distant to reach us.

Too long has the church indulged in disorganized, fly-by-night, individualistic, uncoordinated, do-gooder, one-shot "service projects." It is high time we turned such well-meaning but disastrously naïve efforts into disciplined task forces.

Every church should have not one but two, three, four, and more task forces—to the jail, the ghetto, the nursing homes, the hospitals, the mental hospitals, business, labor, politics, the world, in terms of hosting foreign students and, among other things, resettling refugees.

Churches without such task forces—or their equivalents—have, in my opinion, no business trumpeting the gospel of love. They have no business worshiping a crucified Lord. And they most certainly have no business protesting the entrance of governments and world organizations onto a social scene which they, the churches, have so largely fled.

"Only he who cries out for the Jews," said Bonhoeffer, "has the right to sing Gregorian chant." If you are going to preach, the world is saying to the church, you'd better put your body on the line first if you want anyone to listen.

*   *   *

Then the Church has earned the right to speak. This is the second front of the last discipline. Church members serve through task forces. That's the first front. They also serve by speaking to social issues as they see them, and, I might add, speaking corporately as well as individually.

Things are happening in society. The good things deserve to be praised. The bad things need to be criticized. The church has an obligation to help form the conscience of the society in which it exists. If it's against ghetto housing, let's hear it. If it's against rotten government, let's hear it. If it's for a mental health board, let's hear it. If it's for the good of the many's not being sacrificed to the greed of the few, as happens in many cities, let's hear that too. Otherwise the church by its silence will condone what is bad and deprecate what is good.

Let's not kid ourselves that we have a religion when we haven't the courage of our Christian convictions to put the Christian conscience on record in regard to social issues.

It is nonsense to suggest that there are two moralities, one for Sunday morning and one for the rest of life. The Christian has always fused the moral and the social. That is what has made his religion great. That is what has given his morality blood and his social action sinew. Christ is Lord of the voting booth as well as of the church pew.

What happens when the church is not socially responsible? Karl Marx is what happens. Children were being chained like donkeys to drag the coal out of the coal mines of England, and then Christians wondered why the world got a Karl Marx. Selma is what happens. Watts is what happens. Whatever goes on in your community and my community to frustrate justice is what happens.

The church is a failure when it sees such frustration and does nothing about it. And it is not only a failure, it is an object of contempt. The Nazi propagandist, Goebbels, put that contempt very succinctly when he reportedly said, on behalf of the Nazi party, "Let the churches serve God, we serve the people."

Writing in the *Christian Century,* a Presbyterian elder and former chief editorial writer for the *Minneapolis Tribune* put it this way:

The church has become more of a social institution than a social action institution. . . . If the churches today really are social action institutions, why are they not in the forefront of the battle against social injustice and bigotry? Why are not the churches leading the fight against segregated schools and housing? Why do not the churches fight harder to wipe out discrimination in employment?[10]

The answer is that the church is too often preoccupied with bazaars and men's clubs and flower committees. It is overcommitted and undercommitted. The essential business of the church, going into the world to make disciples of all nations, is lost in a welter of petty institutionalisms as church members wander about aimlessly chanting, "Come weal or come woe, our status is quo."

2

Objections to

a Church that Means Business

Now there are, of course, objections to this particular redis-covery of a cutting edge of the gospel. There are those who do not agree that this is the way the church should organize itself for mission and servanthood.

I

One objection is that the discipline is, in fact, a legalism, and all the arguments which were urged against the Jewish legalism can be urged against this one.

On the contrary, this is nothing at all like a legalism. It has only three rules of the game. The ancient Jews had 613. Some of them, we can only feel, were picayune. The scholar William Barclay, for instance, reports that the Pharisees felt legally bound not to look at women in the streets. Consequently, says Barclay, you had a lot of Pharisees running into walls.

Furthermore, the discipline is simply a spelling out of the vows which churches already have, and the charge of legalism has not, to my knowledge, ever been urged against them.

*

A *second* objection is that the discipline will lead to self-righteousness. If you fulfill your obligation, the objection goes, you will soon feel you have it made and will become smug and intolerable.

The only answer is to say that, in the several years we have been working with the discipline, we have never had a single case of pharisaism. As a matter of fact, it works the other way around. A businessman who goes to the jail says he is sure that he gets far more from the men he visits than they could possibly get from him.

*

A *third* objection is that the standards are too high. It is just unrealistic to expect people to give sacrificially and visit lonely people dying in nursing homes.

If that is true, then we had all better quit. "If any man would come after me, let him deny himself." Christ set the highest possible standard. Surely in our jobs we set the highest possible standards. Surely we like to feel we are setting the highest possible standards for our children. Surely when we go to the doctor we want one with the highest possible standards.

We even have standards in our service organizations. As we have seen, if you miss four times at a Rotary Club you are asked to get with it or get out. That is why you will find men all over the country hurrying to "make up," as they call it, Rotary meetings on Tuesdays. But what happens on Sundays? Men who have not missed a Rotary Club backslapping in eighteen years cannot get to church because they are too busy dropping manure on their flower beds. Why the flowers over the flock? *Because the flock never spelled out its standards.*

We even have standards on the golf course. But do you find the country clubs lowering the par to meet the golfers? Ah, but at least you let the duffer on the course. So does the church. All he has to do is pay his fee. And keep swinging.

*

A *fourth* objection is that the discipline is individualistic. It may work in a young, aggressive middle- to upper-middle-class

congregation, but what about old, torpid upper-class congrega-
tions? What about the inner-city church? The rural church?

On the one hand, the objection is legitimate. What works for
one does not necessarily work for all. Nor should it. Churches
have different styles, just like corporations or any institutions.
Our problem is that we have tried to be all things to all men.
That was Paul's idea. But Paul was a saint. What worked for him
individually does not work for us collectively. There is no reason
why one church should try to be all things to all men. Indeed,
that is *precisely* what has limited our effectiveness. *The* church,
perhaps, should be all things to all men, but not *one* church.
Each church should be faithful to its *own* style. "I was not
disobedient to the heavenly vision," Paul said (Acts 26:19). He
was faithful to his style. And it was some style. It turned the
Jerusalem church off, the Galatian church on.

Every church should be faithful to *its* distinctive style to get
it from where it is to where its Lord wants it to be. The church
is the organization of the Suffering Servant. The *end* of the
church *is* suffering service. *Any* means to reach that end are
legitimate. The end justifies the means. The reason we are in
the malaise we are is that churches either (a) have forgotten the
end of the church, to be a suffering servant, or (b) have not
"done their thing" to get their people there.

But there is more. And the more is that already, in *every*
major Protestant denomination, a minimal discipline *is* in the
church constitution. It is not just a matter of being faithful to our
current style. It is a matter of being faithful to the style that
brought us into being in the first place.

*

A *fifth* objection is that the discipline is exclusivistic.

On the one hand, that is just the point. On the other, our
experience is that less than 5 percent of the people seeking
membership decide not to join the church after presentation of
the discipline. We keep in touch with these people and call on

them later. In the vast majority of cases they were only marginally interested anyway.

*

A *sixth* objection is that the discipline is subjective.

Not so. It is straight out of the Bible and completely consonant with long-established constitutional provisions.

*

A *seventh* objection is that the discipline is premature. Would it not be better to wait until a person is a member before clobbering him with the requirements? Let him get his feet wet. It may take a couple of years, of course—maybe even ten or twenty—before the church member reaches the point where he can really begin to produce, but is it not better to cultivate him on the inside than on the outside?

I think not. This is, of course, the argument that has been used for years by American churches. But I am not impressed with its honesty. I think it is wrong for us to get church members under false pretenses. No one, in my opinion, has any business telling a potential church member that nothing will be required of him when he joins the organization of the Suffering Servant. *It is a contradiction in terms to have a church member who is not also a suffering servant himself.*

It is no good to get people into churches because they "like the minister," or because someone spoke to them gratuitously the first day they came, or because their children like the sandbox. It is no good to get them in that way and then switch the rules on them. They should know the rules from the start. And if they do not like the rules, then they need not join the church.

Furthermore, the argument that the discipline is premature comes with singularly ill grace from businessmen. Certainly no executive would think of hiring someone who was halfhearted. At the very least he wants a man who will show up for work.

You want commitment or you don't want the man. It is the same with the church.

*

An *eighth* objection is that the discipline blocks love.

On the contrary, it releases it. There are always two sides to love, the affectionate and the stormy. God loved Israel, and he showed his love in his discipline as well as in his mercy, in his judgment as well as in his forgiveness. We love our children, and we show our love in our discipline as well as in our affection. A child who receives all affection and no discipline is spoiled. It is then difficult for him, in turn, to love. Furthermore, when we discipline ourselves in churches we are, at last, in a position to *show* our love, to *organize* for it, to see to it that it is *released* regularly in jails and political parties and slums. If a jail visitation can go from 0 to 50 because of discipline, then, frankly, I am for discipline.

*

A *ninth* objection is that the discipline is appropriate only to those who are joining the church. What do you do about those already in?

You do a lot. Our official board has a membership committee. On the committee are the twelve deacons plus the people who call on potential members. We thus have callers for each of our twelve parishes.

The objective of the membership committee is, in the words of the elder in charge, "to challenge St. Luke membership to keep actively and creatively involved in St. Luke's primary emphasis: Study, Share, Serve."

The strategy of the committee is, again in his words, to "1. Demonstrate St. Luke's continuing personal interest in all members; 2. Maintain all necessary parish calls such as birthdays, deaths, hospital calls, calls on the elderly, members who are moving, and so on; 3. Identify specific problem situations where commitment has cooled; 4. Specifically encourage significant involvement by discussing the church's several missions."

If these calls prove unsuccessful, and at least three of them are made over a one-year period, a member who is not enthusiastic about the discipline is asked to join another church. If he fails to do so, he is suspended.

One particular device which we have not yet used but which could be used with great effect is that of publicly reviewing and then renewing one's membership vows every three, say, or five years. Thus you would have people joining and rejoining the church regularly.

*

A *tenth* objection to the discipline is that it is antithetical to justification by faith. It appears to be precisely the opposite, justification by works.

On the contrary. In the first place, Jesus never ruled out work. That is the point about the story of the rich man. He could not do the *work* of selling what he had and giving to the poor. Therefore he did not make the grade with Jesus.

In the second place, as Bonhoeffer has pointed out, there is a difference between costly and cheap grace. His book was called *The Cost of Discipleship*. It is an appropriate title. If the grace in which the Christian stands does not cost him anything, then it really is not grace, is it? After all, the grace in which Christ stood led him to the cross. It cost. If it does not cost, it is not discipleship.

In the third place, the discipline is an effect of love rather than a cause, and there is all the difference in the world between those two positions. A law which *causes* the right relationship with God—justification—is one thing. It is notoriously ineffective. However, a law which is the *result* of a right relationship with God is quite another thing.

It is the difference between Martin Luther on the Spanish

steps in Rome and Martin Luther at the door of the church in Wittenberg. On the first occasion he was going to Rome to get right with God. On the second he felt he *was* right with God, and the 95 Theses were the first step in the proof—the first step, you might say, in his discipline as a disciple.

*

A *final* objection is that the discipline is autocratic. Nazi Germany, the argument goes, was disciplined. The Christian church itself used to be disciplined; there was great involvement by church members, for instance, in the Inquisition.

The objection is semantic. The word "autocratic" is loosely defined and invariably used as a pejorative. One man's autocracy is another man's leadership. One man's autocracy is another man's freedom.

Arguing loosely, there has to be autocracy in any organization. Indeed, there *cannot* be organization without autocracy. Democracy itself cannot function without autocracy. The President of the United States is an autocrat. The president of a company is an autocrat. The head of a family is an autocrat.

Strictly constructed, an autocrat, according to Webster, is "one who rules with undisputed sway." If that is true, Jesus is every Christian's autocrat. The Christian's job is to spell out the demands of the autocracy. One way he does so is to join with people who have the same job. He organizes to spell out the demands of the autocrat. As he organizes he increases his effectiveness.

The organization, however, does *not* "rule with undisputed sway." What it does is *anything* to enable *Jesus* to "rule with undisputed sway." Again, the end justifies the means.

Anything goes to enable Jesus to rule. Anything goes to convert the Chritian into a suffering servant. The church is the organization that will risk everything to do anything to get a man to do *his* thing for Jesus. If that be autocracy, make the most of it.

II

To summarize, I would suggest the following:

One, in the discipline of *study:* that all members of *your* church embark upon some form of regular coming to grips with the Bible and how it relates to job, home, politics, city, country, world.

Two, in the discipline of *sharing:* that all members attend worship weekly, that it be lively, that they be challenged to join a small group, and that they be asked, point-blank, to tithe.

I would further suggest:

A. That an immediate moratorium be placed on all church building by *your* denomination in *your* area which does not stipulate that at least half the money raised be given to starving people, or that it be given to the establishment of low-income housing in your city or to some other meaningful social action program;

B. That no new church in *your* denomination in *your* area be *allowed* to organize if it is not willing from the beginning to split its money 1:2 with starving people—giving away at least half as much as it spends on itself; and to write a clause into its charter calling for a 1:1 split within five years.

C. That *you* issue an encyclical—or whatever it is you issue in your denomination—a postcard, perhaps—*telling* every church in *your* area that it has five years to get its charitable giving up to 1:2; and that it has ten years to get it up to 1:1.

Half the world goes to bed hungry. Six hundred thousand people sleep in the streets of Calcutta. Half the population of Asia, Africa, and Latin America live in unsafe, unhealthful, and overcrowded housing. There is ghetto housing right in our own suburbs. "I was hungry, and you gave me food, I was thirsty and you gave me drink." Not to respond is not only disobedient, it is immoral.

Three, in the discipline of *serving:* I would suggest that every member of *your* church immediately undertake some form of regular 1–to–1 contact with someone who is infintely less fortunate than he. "I was sick and you visited me, I was in prison and you came to me."

I would further suggest that *you* speak as a local church and as a denomination to the desperately important social issues of our day. As Albert Camus, the French atheistic philosopher, put it:

What the world expects of Christians is that [they] should speak out loud and clear, . . . in such a way that never a doubt, never the slightest doubt, could rise in the heart of the simplest man. . . . They should get away from abstraction and confront the bloodstained face history has taken on today.[1]

Four, and last, I would suggest that *your* pastors and boards be given whatever authority is necessary to see to it that these —or similar—goals are sedulously worked at by every church member. I would also suggest that *your* local denominational executives be given whatever authority may be necessary to keep the pastors and councils fighting for the goals.

Local church autonomy and total local church democracy— which is precisely what we have in virtually all our Protestant denominations—is clearly a luxury of the past. We do not have it in our businesses and we do not have it in our governments. We do not have it because it does not work.

It is time to give sufficient power to able men—just as we do in our corporations and just as we do in our governments—to see to it that the plans which are democratically adopted by representative government are effectively followed through.

*

The status can never be quo in a church that means business. Its members realize that a *condition* of church membership is servanthood. A *condition* of church membership is the admission of sin. A *condition* of church membership is the willingness to experiment.

The church is a community of servants. It is a community of sinners. It is a community of scholars. Every church member is called to study. He is called to share. He is called to serve.

And if we have no questions to ask and no sin to admit and no service to give, then we may pledge allegiance to the Man who taught and the Man who forgave and the Man who suffered, but we have no business belonging to that Man's organization.

The church is a club. It is a cadre. It is a highly *ex*clusive organization. To spell out obedience it has vows. To spell out vows it needs a discipline. The status can never be quo in a church that requires its members to study, share, and serve the gospel which we all so blithely profess.

3

The Church and Social Action

For many the church no longer matters. It is no longer an option. It no longer makes a difference. As we have seen, according to the most recent Gallup Poll, 75 percent of Americans say that religion is losing its influence. It is one of the most dramatic shifts, Dr. Gallup reports, in the history of surveys of American life.

One of the reasons for the current disenchantment with the church is that many people see it on the periphery when it should be at the heart. They see it on the outside when it should be on the inside. They see it away from where the action is. In a word, they see the church as oblivious to what is going on around it.

The average American is taxed $402.08 for arms. He is taxed $2.52 for food to feed his fellow citizens.[1] Precisely what has the church said about that? More to the point, what has the church *done* about it?

Seventy-five percent of American Indian families have cash incomes of less than $3,000 a year.[2] What has the church done about *that?*

Thirteen and four-tenths percent of America is *below* the poverty level.[3] That's an urban family of four living on less than $3,300 a year.[4] What has the church done about that?

Fifteen nations have higher literacy rates. Ten nations have lower infant mortality rates. Half the poor have no medical insurance.[5]

By mid-1971 over 44,000 had been killed in Vietnam.[6] It has become necessary to "destroy a town to save it." There is an alleged massacre at Songmy. There is an alleged murder by

24

the Green Berets. There is My Lai.

Our defense budget has doubled every decade. It was $20 billion in 1950, $40 billion in 1960, and $80 billion in 1970.

Six percent of the world, namely America, has 50 percent of the wealth. Six percent of the world will live till the age of 71; the rest of the world will, on the average, be dead before they are 40.[7]

Over 56,000 people a year are killed on the highways, more than half of them by drinking drivers.[8]

The bottom 20 percent of all families received 5 percent of the income in 1946. By 1967 the same 20 percent—now 40 million people—received 5.4 percent of the income. Meanwhile the top 5 percent receive 20 percent.[9]

We could go on, but what's the use? The point is, there are social problems in America. And the question is, *are we going to address ourselves to them as churches or are we not?*

I

One answer is that we are not. In its most extreme form this is the answer of *apathy*. Apathy comes from the Greek for "without feeling." We do not feel for those less fortunate. We do not feel for victims of injustice. In Jesus' parable of the Good Samaritan, we pass by on the other side.

Unfortunately there are a good many church members who, for one reason or another, hold the apathetic position. It is not the business of the church, they say, to be involved in social issues. That is the business of the political party. It is the business of the chamber of commerce and the liquor lobby. But it is not the business of the church.

On the contrary, it is precisely this reasoning which is responsible for the morass in which we find ourselves. It is precisely the divorce of the church from the mainstream of life that has helped bring the tragic statistics upon us.

The church fled to the suburbs because church members

wanted to get away from it all. They wanted to leave the social issues behind. They wanted to live in a microcosm of the kingdom of God in which the major enemy was crabgrass.

In my experience, people who live in suburbs are often self-centered, insular, antimetropolitan, and afflicted with a boundless determination to keep taxes down and undesirables out. Consequently their churches tend to be quiet. They tend to be isolationist. They tend to pass by on the other side. It was the middle-class religious establishment in Jesus' story who passed by on the other side.

But it is not just the suburbs. A study has been completed through the National Opinion Research Center at the University of Chicago which reveals a portrait of the American churchgoer as

one who has a self-centered preoccupation with saving his own soul, an alienated, other-worldly orientation coupled with an indifference toward—even a tacit endorsement of—a social system that would perpetuate social inequality and injustice.[10]

We have a national picture, in other words, of a church that passes by on the other side.

One reason for the apathy has been our infatuation with psychology and our neglect of sociology. We have talked about "the power of positive thinking" but we have not talked about "the power of positive acting." We have talked too much and done too little. We have spent too much time on "as yourself" and too little time on "Love your neighbor." Consequently the response of no response to social problems could have been predicted.

But now, in the 1970's, it is a serious matter. The church is going to be made or broken to the extent that it can get off its psychological island and back into the mainstream of life. This is *not* a denigration of psychology. It *is* a denigration of psychology at the *expense* of sociology. We must restore the balance. How it got out of whack in the first place is a mystery. You rarely find Jesus talking about the self. You almost invariably find him talking about the self in relation to others or the self in relation to God. One is tempted to think that the balance was upset by apathetic American Christians going their pietistic, individualistic, salvationistic way, steadfastly refusing to be involved.

It's amazing [writes Dick Gregory] how we come to this church every Sunday and cry over the crucifixion of Christ, and we don't cry over these things that are going on around and among us. If He was here now and saw these things, He would cry. And He would take those nails again. For us.[11]

Apathy is a copout. Apathy is sin.

II

Another response to social problems is *sympathy*. It comes from the Greek for "feeling with" or "feeling like." We feel with the other guy. We cross the road. We read the statistics with compassion.

The religious universe is by no means peopled solely with apathists. There are sympathists as well. Plenty of them. These are the people who tutor in ghetto schools. They are the people who man the hot lines. They are the people who go to the jails and hospitals and nursing homes.

Such people care very much. They do not look at the world with dry eyes. They get involved. They get so involved that the tears of another become their tears. The laughter of another becomes their laughter.

It is a beautiful thing to watch, this movement from apathy to sympathy, which is why Jesus told his story. And he deliberately drew the story lines so that the two men would be as far apart as possible. He wanted to make sure that it was next to impossible for the one man to feel with or like the other. He made them enemies. Jews and Samaritans hated each other.

There are those who will stop by the side of the road. The family that took in the thief. The family that took in the addict.

The man who said he had the first religious experience of his life with a lonely young man in a jail. The men and women who stay up until one and two in the morning to talk with young people in trouble. The young people themselves who get into cars and go off to nursing homes and the reformatory.

But is that enough? Is that kind of personal involvement in social problems enough? It is beautiful as far as it goes, but does it go far enough?

This is not to criticize sympathy. Far from it. Sympathy is essential. What do the figures mean if I don't know an Indian? If I don't know a poor person? If I don't know a black, a young person on dope, an enemy—a Black Panther, a John Bircher, a member of SDS—broken by the side of the road?

Sympathy is essential. But is it enough?

III

There is a third response to social problems. It is *empathy*. Empathy comes from the Greek for "feeling in." You feel with or feel like the other guy so much that you feel you are *in his place*. "Great Spirit," reads a Sioux Indian prayer, "let me not criticize another man until I have walked in his moccasins for two weeks." With empathy, with Christian *agape*, you are *in* the other guy's moccasins.

What does that mean? It means that you care so much about him that you move beyond personal response to his problem to social response. You move beyond personal involvement to corporate involvement. You move beyond social service to social action.

Surely the high point of feeling is not to take a food basket to a hungry family at Christmas. It is to work *as a church* to eliminate the conditions which produce the hunger.

Surely the high point of feeling is not to visit a lonely young man in jail. It is to work *as a church* to reform a penal system so primitive that its primary tool for correcting behavior is still punishment.

Surely the high point of feeling is not just to mourn one who has been killed by a drunk driver. It is to do all in your power *as a church* to demand that your state legislature eliminate the drunk-driver scourge from our roads.

Surely the high point of feeling is not just to say a few words at the funeral of a friend dead on arrival at General Hospital from an overdose of heroin, but to do all in your power *as a church* to move your community to eliminate the conditions that helped to produce her unimaginable alienation and despair.

* * *

How do we do it? We *organize* our love. That is the way love is going to be effective in the America of 1971, 1972, and beyond. It is one thing to tutor a child on the floor in a slum school. It is another thing to organize a hundred of your friends —namely, your *church*—to go to your state legislator and demand—not ask, but demand—more adequate funds for inner-city education, and then stick to him, *as a church*, until he gets the funds.

The time has come for corporate solutions to corporate problems. The time has come to move beyond apathy to sympathy and beyond sympathy to empathy. If we *really* feel for the other guy we will organize our love to eliminate his distress— not minister to it, but eliminate it.

The trouble is that it is not only the apathists who are the copouts. Sympathists are copouts too. Any man in a church who says he is concerned about the 6 percent unemployment figure, but then in the same breath says he is only middle management and therefore can *do* nothing about it, is a copout. Any man in a church who makes $18,000 a year manufacturing food for families who can afford it and yet does not have time to organize his fellow executives to do something about families who cannot afford his food, is a copout. And any man in front of a congregation who makes his living chastising and loving it and yet does not get down to the nitty-gritty of *organizing* it for social action, is a copout, too.

Social service is not enough. A church must never be lulled into thinking that because a few of its members have visited in a reformatory they have *done* anything for juvenile delinquency. For juvenile delinquents, yes—one or two, here and there—but for juvenile delinquency, basically no. The final measure of success of all a church's social service is how far it has led that church into social action. That is, *to what extent has the church changed the structures of society which helped to create the social evil in the first place?*

This is the other balance that must be restored in the seventies or it will be all over for the church. That Gallup Poll figure is going up every year. Not only must the psychological at last be balanced by the sociological. The 1-to-1 in the sociological must at last be balanced by the group-to-group. The personal dimension of love must be balanced by the social. If it is not, then the church—the young, the poor, the black, and the dispossessed are telling us—will be in major trouble.

* * *

Fortunately, however, the church has some things going for it. They are major sources of inspiration. They have worked before, and there is no reason why they should not work now.

First, there is Jesus himself. Jesus took on the group. This is not *all* he did. But it is *part* of what he did. He engaged in social action. He loved *so much* that he moved beyond personal to corporate involvement. That was the *point* of the cross, the greatest symbol of empathy in the history of the world. That was the *point* of the entry into Jerusalem. He could have come alone; instead he organized a street demonstration and took on the whole city. That was the *point* of his throwing the economic, religious, social, and political establishment out of the temple. He could have preached a sermon; instead he organized a coup. It worked. It worked so well that they called him a rabble-rouser, an agitator, a radical. And they specifically asked that he be executed for "stirring up the people" (Luke 23:5). Order, in other words—a word we hear so often today—over justice.

When Jesus talked about God it was all right. But when he got specific and began talking about men, and about how people were going to have to be changed if the buried men were ever to be found, then the establishment had to react. And they reacted as most establishments do: they called the cops. Every city has its Pilate: its mayor or its city attorney or any in its populace so obsessed with order that they forget justice.

The irony is that it was all there to begin with, if they had only listened. Jesus' first sermon, in his home town, was a straight-out social action sermon.

> The Spirit of the Lord is upon me [he quoted Isaiah],
>   because he has anointed me to preach good news to the *poor.*
> He has sent me to proclaim release to the *captives*
>   and recovering of sight to the *blind,*
> to set at liberty those who are *oppressed,*
>   to proclaim the acceptable year of the Lord.*
>
>   (Luke 4:18–19)

But they couldn't take it, and they threw him out of town.

Second, as Jesus implied, there are the prophets. Social action comes from the Old Testament as well as the New. It is a cornerstone of the Hebrew tradition. The prophets were a task force on national goals. They were the champions of the young, the poor, the different, the dispossessed.

> Did not your father eat and drink
>   and do *justice* and *righteousness?* . . .
> He judged the cause of the *poor* and *needy.* . . .
> Is not *this* to know me?
>   says the Lord.
>
>   (Jer. 22:15–16)

---

*Emphasis added to quotations from modern sources is acknowledged in the Notes. I have, however, also italicized wording that seems especially relevant throughout the Biblical passages, without comment other than this note.

> Seek *justice*,
>   correct *oppression;*
> defend the *fatherless*,
>   plead for the *widow*.
>   (Isa. 1:17)

> I hate, I despise your feasts,
>   and I take no delight in your solemn assemblies. . . .
> Take away from me the noise of your songs;
>   to the melody of your harps I will not listen.
> But let *justice* roll down like waters,
>   and *righteousness* like an everflowing stream.
>   (Amos 5:21, 23–24)

> He has showed you, O man, what is good;
>   and what does the Lord *require* of you
> but to do *justice*, and to love kindness,
>   and to walk humbly with your God?
>   (Mic. 6:8)

With Christ and the prophets a church can go far in social action. If it does not, then it is not a church.

4

Objections to
the Church and Social Action

We have said that it is necessary for churches to take social action. We must also say *why* it is necessary.

Perhaps the best way to say *why* social action is necessary is by responding to those who say it is *not* necessary. At least this method hangs out all the wash, if nothing else, and it may give us a primer for answering the stock objections to church involvement in social issues.

I

A *first* objection is that the church should mind its own business. Its proper business is God, Jesus, the Bible, Sunday School, and so on. It is improper for the church to be involved in the great social issues of this day.

This is to say, in effect, that the province of the church is ends, not means. The Bible tells us about love, justice, brotherhood, peace. But it does not tell us how to achieve them. Therefore the church should stick to preaching man's dreams. But it should not be concerned with how to put those dreams into action.

Unfortunately this is a totally inadequate reading of the Bible. Abraham had a dream of the Promised Land. The Bible records how he got there. The prophets had a dream about justice. The Bible records how they spelled that dream out. Jesus had a dream about brotherhood. The Bible records how he spelled his dream out. Precisely the reason the Bible has stuck is that it is a document of ends *and* means. Christianity sticks because it fastens a man to big dreams and then annoys him until he puts those dreams into action. It tells a man where he is. It tells him where he ought to be. And it tells him how to get there.

What use is a dream about brotherhood if I *do* nothing to bring about brotherhood? What use is a dream about peace if I *do* nothing to bring about peace?

The *point* of religion is low-income housing in the suburbs. The *point* of religion is how much money a company makes on illegal fragmentation bombs.

It is a copout not to spell out. Religion *is* the action as well as the dream. Religion *is* the means as well as the ends. Religion *is* the ethics as well as the theology. "How can a man love God whom he has not seen," Jesus asked, "if he does not love his brother whom he has seen?"

The church's job is precisely to get *more* specific rather than less. The church's *job* is morality. The church's *job* is ethics. The church's *job* is to step into the moral vacuum in our country and spell out its vision of God in terms of its action for justice. "I was hungry and you gave me food; I was thirsty and you gave me drink."

*

A *second* objection to social action by churches is that the church's job is to deal with man's spiritual life. It is not to deal with his political life. Its proper sphere is worship and all that worship entails. It is most certainly not corporate action and all that it entails.

Again we are involved in a misreading of the Judeo-Christian tradition. It is not enough to limit religion to "spirit" any more than it is enough to limit religion to "ends." The Judeo-Christian tradition does not split man apart in this fashion. Indeed, it is the genius of our religion that it holds man together, as opposed to the Greek heresy and the Manichean heresy and other religions which say that a man's soul is good and his body bad. The purpose of these religions is to get out of the body and into the soul. But that is most emphatically *not* the purpose of the Judeo-Christian religion. God made the world, we are told in Genesis, and the world was "good."

However, there is more, and the more is that this is entirely too narrow a definition of spirit. The church is told to stick to spiritual matters. But is not concern for the victims of injustice, asks the former Secretary General of the World Council of Churches, a *most* spiritual matter? Is not concern for the victims of war a *most* spiritual matter? Is not concern for the overweening nationalism that causes most wars a *most* spiritual matter?

Talk about worship,

> Is not *this* the fast that I choose:
>   to loose the bonds of wickedness,
>   to undo the thongs of the yoke,
> to let the oppressed go free,
>   and to break every yoke?
> Is it not to share your bread with the hungry,
>   and bring the homeless poor into your house?
>   (Isa. 58:6–7)

That *is* worship—not to sit in church caressing your spirit, but to get out there and *do* something about oppression. To worship *is* to work for justice. Do you know the church with the most beautiful liturgy? It is the Russian Orthodox, and they sat by while the Communists took over their country.

Let it never be said that the church deals with the soul while the state deals with the body. Jesus Christ is Lord of *all* life, we are told again and again in the New Testament. "The heart of Christianity," said the great Indian Christian, D. T. Niles, "is not concern for the soul but concern for the world." "For God so loved the *world*. . . ." "God was in Christ reconciling the *world* to himself."

*

A *third* objection to social action by churches is that the church's job is individual salvation. Change men one by one, and then you will change society. But stick to your job of changing men.

Again, the objection is a gross distortion of the Christian position. To be sure, the Christian religion is concerned with personal salvation. But that is not *all* it is concerned with. Indeed, a good case could be made for personal salvation's being *secondary* in the Christian religion to social salvation. Love God. Love neighbor. That is the Judeo-Christian position. God first, others second, self *last.*

Individual salvation was precisely the position of the Lutheran Church in Lutheran Germany during the rise of Hitler. The Lutheran Church preached a personal and not a social gospel. The consequences, as we all know, were horrendous.

They came first for the Communists [wrote the German pastor, Martin Niemoller] and I didn't speak up because I wasn't a Communist. Then they came for the Jews, and I didn't speak up because I wasn't a Jew. Then they came for the trade unionists, and I didn't speak up because I wasn't a trade unionist. Then they came for the Catholics, and I didn't speak up because I was a Protestant. Then they came for me, and by that time there was no one left to speak up.[1]

It is utterly illusory to tell the church to stick to individual salvation. Obviously, if every soul were saved society would be too. But every soul is not saved. And things are happening in society to prevent salvation. War is one. Racism is another. Pitiful welfare budgets another.

It is most interesting that in all dictatorship countries the church is told to stick to individual salvation. It is equally interesting that in America the radical right in politics allies itself with the radical right in religion and tells the church to stick to individual salvation.

But how are individuals going to be cured when their envi-

ronment is full of disease? It can be done, and that is one side
of the truth. But it cannot always be done, or even regularly
done, and that is the other side.

The cure of souls is enormously affected by what goes on in
politics, economics, education. Therefore the Christian had better affect what is going on. There is something hollow about a
country-club Christian telling a ghetto delinquent to "love his
Jesus." Eliminate the ghetto and you may eliminate the delinquent.

Let us not go out to save individuals one by one while our
society is being lost thousands by thousands. Let us move from
love of self to love of neighbor. Let us get over our romantic
eighteenth-century frontier individualism and get back into the
prophetic mainstream of corporate action on corporate issues.

*

A *fourth* objection to social action by churches is that it's OK
for individuals but wrong for groups. The individual Christian
can do all the social action he wants, but he must not do it with
other Christians as a local church.

Why not? Because the church will become another political
party? But it won't, and we all know that it won't. That's a
dodge. The church has no interest whatever in supplanting the
two-party system.

Because the church will become a pressure group? Why *not*
become a pressure group? Why *not* press for spelling love out
in justice? It is precisely because the church *refused* to press for
justice in America that we got into the mess we did in 1861.
That isn't the only reason, but it is certainly one reason. It was
OK for individual Christians in the senate and elsewhere to do
whatever they wanted to do about justice. But it was wrong for
the church as the *church* to do anything about justice. "I fear
the silence of the churches," said Martin Luther King, "more
than the shouts of the angry multitudes."

What about the violence of poverty? What about the violence

of hunger? What about the violence of war? Are we going to be silent about our violences the way the 1861 church was silent? Or will we speak?

The individual voice is not enough. It is utterly simplistic to leave the entire struggle for justice in the hands of Christians individually. We do not do that sort of thing in our businesses and we do not do it in our governments. We do not do it because it does not work. It is time for a corporate voice on corporate matters.

If the old way had worked, that would be one thing. But it has patently not worked. Individual action for corporate justice is not enough. We need corporate action for corporate justice.

If you pour yourself out to the hungry [Isaiah said to the "church"]
   and satisfy the desire of the afflicted,
then shall your light rise in the darkness
   and your gloom be as the noonday.

(Isa. 58:10)

The church is the body of Christ. Just as individual salvation is not enough, so individual social action is not enough. We do together what we cannot do as well alone.

*

A *fifth* objection to social action by churches is that it will "split the church down the middle." It is not worth it, the objection goes, to risk tearing the church apart by working for social justice.

On the contrary: that is precisely the risk that *is* worth taking. It is the risk that *must* be taken if the church is going to make it through the seventies. It is really a question of what you want: a divided church that stands for something or a united church that stands for nothing.

But it is not that simple. I am not persuaded that social action is nearly as divisive as we may think. We really haven't *tried* social action, so we are not in a position, in most of our churches, to make this assumption. As the late G. K. Chesterton put it: "It is not that Christianity has been tried and found wanting. It has been found difficult and so never really tried."

But if there is tension, is not this *precisely* the creative tension we *should* be creating? Is not the deployment of the ABM *precisely* the kind of question we should be discussing in, of all places, churches—where we are concerned about spelling our love out in justice? Let us have forums to discuss these questions monthly, if not weekly.

Creative conflict was the *point* of Lexington Common. It was the *point* of the Christians in the arenas. It was the *point* of Jesus taking on the establishment at every turn.

The trouble is that the middle class wants to *avoid* conflict. It *is* the silent majority. It *wants* to be silent. It is time the church became the leaven in the middle-class lump. It is time to *create* conflict for love. Jesus was always creating conflict for love. How can we know peace without conflict? "They have healed the wound of my people lightly," Jeremiah warned, "saying 'Peace, peace,' when there is no peace."

Conflict is the *way* to reconciliation. That is why Jesus chose it. Division is the *way* to unity. That is why Jesus chose it. The beautiful thing is that if we are united by our love for him we can withstand any conflict. More to the point, we can grow in love *because* of the conflict. "I have not come to bring peace, but a sword." "He *is* our peace."

*

A *sixth* objection to social action by churches is that it distorts the church's total program. It turns the church into another social service agency like the United Fund or another social action agency like the gun lobby.

But this of course is not true. It is a caricature. The fact of the matter is that a church's social action is one-half of one-third of its total effort. The church studies—the *kerygma* of the first church. The church shares—the *koinonia* of the first church. And the church serves—the *diakonia* of the first church. Any one to the exclusion of the others distorts the church's business.

The danger really is not that the church becomes a cadre. It is that the church *has* become a study group. It *has* become a social group, but not a social action group. To get the balance back, it is very possible that social action *will* have to be emphasized for a while. Then the church will learn to study, share, and serve in roughly equal proportions.

*

A *seventh* objection to social action by churches is that churches should be neutral. They should not take sides. They should be above civil strife. "The Holy See," writes Rolf Hochhuth in his scathing play, *The Deputy*, "must remain a haven for the spirit of neutrality."

But is that so? It is precisely the Pope's neutrality, says Hochhuth, that helped to murder the Jews in the Second World War. How can a man standing in the tradition of Amos, Jeremiah, Isaiah, Jesus, say that the church has no right to speak out against injustice? *The question is not what right does the church have to speak, but what right does the church have to be silent?*

Silence is consent. To be silent *is* to speak. It is to agree with what is going on. To be neutral *is* to act. It is to favor no action, which is an action in favor of the status quo. The issue, then, is *not* whether we take sides, but *which* side we will take. The issue is *not* whether we will speak, but *what* we will say.

> Cry aloud, spare not,
>   lift up your voice like a trumpet. . . .
>   (Isa. 58:1)

God *is* what moves us to social action.

*

An *eighth* objection to social action by churches is that it violates the familiar position of "faith alone." It appears to be the opposite—namely, "works alone."

Unfortunately the "faith alone" position, although familiar, is heretical. It is an overemphasis on one aspect of the truth, which is what a heresy is. It was a needed overemphasis at the time of Luther to correct a disastrous imbalance. But now it in turn must be balanced.

Jesus never ruled out work. The Good Samaritan did a good work. Jesus "went about doing good." "By their fruits you shall know them," he said. "Faith without works," said a later New Testament writer, "is dead." "Let us consider," wrote another, "how to *stir up* one another to love and good works."

The church's *job* is to spell out its faith in works. The church's *job* is to stir people up to love. Indeed, to restore the imbalance in the seventies we might even say the church's job is to get people to do the right things *more* than it is to get them to think the right thoughts.

Works *before* faith. What we *do* determines what we think. You can often act yourself into a new way of thinking more readily than you can think yourself into a new way of acting.

In the South, the number of people who would object to sending their children to school with colored children has declined from 72 per cent in 1958 to 37 per cent by 1965.[2]

What happened? There was a Supreme Court decision desegregating the schools. And there was social action by Martin Luther King, Jr. Change the behavior, in other words, and you will change the belief. "Beliefs change more slowly," reads a scientific finding, "than actual behavior."[3] As John Dewey put it, people "learn what they live."

*

A *ninth* objection to social action by churches is that it should be left to the politicians, to those elected and to those who are seeking election.

But who are the politicians? They are church members, many if not most of them. Do they not want to have their judgments informed by the collective judgment of their church?

Politics is too important to be left to politicians, just as war is too important to be left to generals. In a democracy politics is everybody's business. The very word "politics" comes from the Greek word for "citizen." That makes us all politicians.

More to the point: the Greek word for "church" was the *same* as the word for "public service." And a special name was reserved by the Greeks for anyone who refused to take part in public affairs. He was called an "idiot."

Even if we were able to leave politics to the politicians, it wouldn't work because the sad fact of the matter is there are too few of them. Despite such brave sentiments as "we are all politicians," the facts, according to a 1968 University of Michigan study, are:

> Out of every 100 registered voters
> only 8 attend political meetings of any kind;
> only 7 give money to a campaign;
> only 5 belong to a party organization;
> only 3 do other work for either candidate or party.

By contrast:

> Out of every 100 Americans
> 63 will belong to churches and
> 21 will serve as working members.

It can only be concluded that the cause of social justice is not served by leaving it to party politics alone. "Let your manner of life," Paul wrote, "be worthy of the gospel of Christ" (Phil. 1:27). It meant literally "behave as citizens."

*

A *tenth* objection to social action by churches is that "you can't legislate morality." Therefore churches should stay out of trying to influence legislation or change community conduct.

Surely this has to be one of the great fictions of all time. It is amazing how such vapid clichés relieve us of the need to think. The fact of the matter is that laws are precisely attempts to legislate morality. They are attempts to regulate behavior. How

I behave *is* my morality. My morality *is* how I relate to other people.

I do not go through a red light because there is a law against it. There is a law against it because it is dangerous behavior. The law says in effect that it is immoral to threaten the life of another by going through a red light. Therefore citizens will not go through red lights.

"The idea that you cannot legislate morality—civilized behavior—" said Justice Goldberg, "is a foolish, nonsensical idea." "As we noted in our Sunday Law decisions," wrote Justice Brennan, "nearly every criminal law on the books can be traced to some religious principle or inspiration."

> What does the Lord *require* of you
> but to do *justice* . . . ?
> (Mic. 6:8)

It was a legal term. And it meant a particular kind of legality. To judge righteously meant in the Old Testament a legal system that would give back right to those from whom it had been taken—namely, the poor and the oppressed.[4]

*

An *eleventh* objection to social action by churches is that it violates the separation of church and state.

But does it? No one is talking about a Christian political party. No one is talking about a state church or a church state. Separation of church and state, yes; separation of religion and politics, no.

America is founded on religion. The Pilgrims came for religion. "Religion and morality," Washington said, "are the indispensable supports of freedom." "One nation, under God" we specifically add to the Pledge of Allegiance. "In God we trust" we put on our money.

I for my part [said President Wilson] would not wish to see *any* church run *any* community, but I do wish to see *every* church assist the community in which it is established to run itself, to show that the spirit of Christianity is the spirit of assistance, of vitalization, of intense interest in *everything* that affects the lives of men and women and children.[5]

*

A *twelfth* objection to social action by churches is that the action the church takes may turn out to be wrong. Look at the Inquisition.

Fortunately this is true. The church is not always right. What has to be weighed is the risk of action vs. the risk of inaction. Today the risk of action is great, but that of inaction is greater. Again, the question is not: What right does the church have to act? It is: What right does the church have *not* to act?

A do-nothing church just simply is not going to be tolerated in the seventies. Ask the young. Ask the poor. Ask the black. Ask the world. It is time to risk. If the old way of no-risk had worked, that would be one thing. But it has not worked. It is time now to risk much that we may win much.

The church [writes ethics professor Roger Shinn] . . . has erred more often by a silence that meant a tacit support of the establishment than by deeds of ethical daring.[6]

Put another way:

Life [said Justice Holmes] is action and passion. It is required of a man that he should share the passion and action of his time at peril of being judged not to have lived.[7]

Put another way, and perhaps most succinctly:

Behold the turtle—he makes progress only as he sticks his neck out.

*

A *thirteenth* objection to social action by churches is that the action is not agreeable to everyone. "They don't speak for me" you invariably hear.

Maybe they don't. It would be surprising indeed if everyone

agreed on everything. That kind of conformity is neither helpful nor sought. Anywhere from 30 percent to 49.9 percent of
the voters will disagree with many of the actions taken by their
congressman, whom the other 50.1 percent elected. Many of
the 50.1 percent will also disagree.

Nevertheless action is taken. It does not wait upon unanimity.
The duly elected representatives of the people—in the copora-
tion, the government, the church, the lodge, the PTA—vote
their convictions and move their body ahead.

Jesus did not wait for public opinion to crystallize before
entering Jerusalem. He entered. He did what he felt he had to
do. His action obviously did not speak *for* everyone in the
church. But it most certainly spoke *to* them. He ran the risk of
offending a great many people. It was a risk worth running. His
action still speaks.

However, having said this, as indicated earlier the chances
are excellent that on many social issues tackled by the church
unanimity will be close. "They don't speak for me" is often an
academic objection not founded in experience.

*

A *fourteenth* objection to social action by churches is that the
action is always "liberal." It represents one side of the political
spectrum to the exclusion of the other.

But does it? What is liberal or conservative about a four-lane
highway through the heart of a lake? What is liberal or conservative about a man who is vilified for going to a meeting of
socialists? What is liberal or conservative about a war that has
been waged by both liberals and conservatives?

"Do justice." To repeat: it meant case law. Case law meant
restoring community. Restoring community meant giving back
right to those from whom it had been taken—namely, the poor
and the oppressed.

It was the great conservative Robert Taft who became an
early champion of low-income housing. It was the great con-

servative Edmund Burke who said: "The only thing necessary for evil to triumph is for enough good men to do nothing." When men are united for justice, whatever their label, community can be restored.

*

A *final* objection to social action by churches is that, even granting that social action may be good, I am not ready for it. I don't have the time. It's not my thing.

That may be, but perhaps it should be your thing more than you think. We generally have time for what we feel is important, and if we say we have no time for social action, then we are saying we do not feel it is important.

If a man is not ready for social action he would do well to get ready because social action is without question the name of the game for the church in the seventies. Without dramatic evidence that the church cares, the church as we know it just simply is not going to make it out of the decade.

One of the best ways to get ready for social action is through social service. When I know someone who is poor, I am more likely to do all in my power for the 13.4 percent of America who are *below* the poverty level.

For others the step of social service before social action will not be necessary. They know the inequities. They read the statistics with compassion. They have experienced or seen injustice. All they want is to act. They want to work for justice. They want to restore community. They want to spell their love out to the farthest possible extent.

If it isn't *our* thing, whose is it? If *we* don't have time for justice, who does? If white, Anglo-Saxon, Protestant, middle-class America is the *silent* majority, who will speak? The young radicals? The John Birchers? The Communists?

The very *least* we can do is try what we haven't tried and do what we haven't done, and move corporately now for corporate solutions to corporate disasters.

The very *least* we can do is organize now for social justice by belonging to an organization that makes a difference, that is on the inside rather than the outside, that is where the action is.

As the great Frenchman, de Tocqueville, reportedly put it after his visit to America more than a century ago,

I sought for the greatness and the genius of America in her commodious harbors and her ample rivers, and it was not there. . . . In the fertile fields and boundless forests, and it was not there. . . . In her public school system and her institutions of learning, and it was not there. . . . In her democratic congress and matchless constitution, and it was not there.

Not until I went into the churches of America and heard her pulpits flame with righteousness did I understand the secret of her genius and power. America is great because America is good, and if America ever ceases to be good, America will cease to be great.

5

The Church and Justice

It is one thing to say a church must be involved in social action. It is another to define *what* that action should be. It is one thing to say with Isaiah, "Seek justice." It is another to define what justice is. It is one thing to pledge allegiance to "justice for all." It is another thing to spell out what the Bible—not Jefferson, not John Stuart Mill, not Plato—meant by justice.

I

The Bible does *not* mean rendering every man his due. It does not mean conduct befitting an ethical or legal norm. It does not mean majority rule. It does not mean the preservation of order. It does not mean the greatest good for the greatest number.

Justice—or "righteousness"—in the Bible means *fulfilling the demands of a relationship.*[1] It means establishing *community.* It means getting for the other guy what you have already gotten for yourself. It means giving the other guy what you have already been given. It means thinking of the other guy *first.*

That which is right in a legal sense is that which fulfils the demands of the community relationship, and the sole function of the judge is to maintain the community, to restore right to those from whom it has been taken.[2]

The just man is thus the man who fights for the rights of the poor. He is the man who defends the oppressed, who cares for

48

the widow and the orphan, who goes out of his way to help the helpless and be a voice for the voiceless.

> Seek justice,
> correct oppression;
> defend the fatherless,
> plead for the widow.
> (Isa. 1:17)

The genius of the prophets was that they did not mince. They called a spade a spade. They would not let the rich in the synagogue ignore the poor. They would not let a man who had it made turn his back on a man who was struggling to make it. As Rousseau observed, nations are judged by what happens to the man at the bottom of the ladder.

> Woe to those who decree iniquitous decrees
>   and the writers [of laws] who keep writing oppression,
> to turn aside the needy from justice
>   and to rob the poor of my people of their right,
> that widows may be their spoil,
>   and that they may make the fatherless their prey!
> (Isa. 10:1–2)

It is the same in the New Testament. Jesus has no time for the exploiters. His sharpest criticism is directed against the church establishment. Why? Because they were smug. They were indifferent to the needs of others. It was the church establishment in his story that passed by on the other side. It was the church establishment that killed *him*.

Jesus is just because he fulfills the demands of relationship. He is in relationship to God and he fulfills the relation's demands. He is obedient. It is the same with others. He is in relationship to every other human being. If they are sons of the same father then they are brothers. Brothers are in relationship. "Love your neighbor" was Jesus' equivalent of Isaiah's "Seek justice."

Jesus is not just because he obeys a moral norm.[3] He is just because he is a servant: he is obedient to the demands of his relationship to God and he is obedient to the demands of his relationship to others. Indeed, he is *not* obedient to what is usually thought of as the ethical or even legal norm.

The Son of man has come eating and drinking; and you say, "Behold, a glutton and a drunkard, a friend of tax collectors and sinners!" (Luke 7:34)

> Behold my servant . . .
> he will bring forth *justice* to the nations.
> (Isa. 42:1)

Justice means fulfilling the demands of a relationship. It means establishing community. It means a church getting for the other guy what they, the church members, have already gotten for themselves. It means giving the other guy what they have already been given themselves. It means thinking of the other guy *first—before* they budget for the heat and the light and the paid soloists.

II

There are, then, the following attributes of justice:

One, it is aggressive. Not, of course, in the sense of being hostile, but in the sense of being bold. Justice takes the initiative. It does not just sit back and decide between initiatives others have taken. It does not merely weigh both sides of the scales. *It weights one side of the scales so that the rights of the one may at last be equal to the rights of the other.*

Thus righteousness as a forensic concept is *not* an impartial decision between two parties, based on a legal norm, such as is known in Western law, but *protecting, restoring, helping righteousness, which helps those who have had their right taken from them in the communal relationship to regain it.*[4]

Justice is aggressive. It is not enough to arbitrate; it must advocate. "*Seek* justice." "What does the Lord require of you but to *do* justice?" "Let justice *roll down* like waters." The word for justice meant law. To do justice meant to do *your* part in fulfilling the demands of the relationship *you* had with someone who did *not* have as much as *you*. It meant for rulers of religious communities to pass laws which would restore right to those from whom it had been taken.

In 1966 we broke our oldest treaty with the Indians, made in 1794 with the Senecas.[5] In 1969 we paid a man $146,792 not to grow cotton, while we paid the people who live on his plantation $35.00 a month in relief.[6] We spend for research in mental health one tenth of what we spend for chewing gum.[7] We spend at the federal level

$3.4 billion for space, but $1.4 billion for housing; $7.3 billion for weapons research, but $1.4 billion for higher education; $540 million for a nuclear aircraft carrier, but $200 million for parks and open space.[8]

How aggressive *are* churches for justice? What ever *happened* to the Kerner Report? Where *is* the middle-income housing? Where *is* the medical care for the poor? Who *is* defending the defenseless?

The weak you have not strengthened, the sick you have not healed, the crippled you have not bound up, the strayed you have not sought, and with force and harshness you have ruled them. (Ezek. 34:4)

The future of this country is *precisely* a matter of whether those in churches who have more will be aggressive for those —in or out of churches—who have less. It is *precisely* a matter of whether church members will get for the other what they have already gotten for themselves. It is a matter of whether they will think of the other guy *first*.

III

Two, justice is divisive. Its end may be unity but its means are division. You cannot say what needs to be said to churches to get them to do what needs to be done without agreement by some and disagreement by others. Not always but often.

> The Lord enters into *judgment*
> with the elders and princes of his people:
> "It is *you* who have devoured the vineyard,
> the spoil of the poor is in your houses.
> What do you mean by crushing my people,
> by grinding the face of the poor?"
>
> (Isa. 3:14–15)

That's divisive.

Division is healthy. Division is common. Every time a bill is passed some will be for it and some against. Every time an attempt is made to restore community some will favor and some will oppose it.

It can then be objected that we will destroy our churches in order to save them, that we will destroy community in the name of justice, that we will divide so much that we cannot unite. But is that so? Or is division the *way* to unity? Is disunity the *way* to community?

Take my community. It may have been divided over sex education. But now there may be more unity before over the need for excellence in the public schools. Because of temporary disunity the cause of community may have inched ahead.

Take our country. We were divided in 1861 over slavery. But now there may be more unity than before over the need for aggressive justice. Temporary division served ultimate unity.

Be that as it may, the major division is not *between* us so much as *within* us. We are divided within ourselves over the very possibility of community itself. One part of us says you are *never* going to get anybody to put the other guy first. The other part of us says you *must* put the other guy first. One part says you are *never* going to get people to act in someone else's interest. The other part says you *must* get people to act in the other's interest. One part of us says we are *selfish*. The other part says we are *selfless*.

It is the old division St. Paul felt, only he wasn't as delicate in his choice of words. He called it a war.

I find it to be a law that when I want to do right, evil lies close at hand. For I delight in the law of God, in my inmost self, but I see in my members another law at *war* with the law of my mind and making me captive to the law of sin. . . . (Rom. 7:21–23)

Madison carried it a step further. As far as he was concerned, the war was won. The selfish beat the selfless. Society was simply a congeries of self-interests. Justice was giving first one dominance, then another.

The causes of faction *cannot* be removed and . . . relief is *only* to be sought in the means of controlling its effects. . . . The latent causes of faction are thus sown in the nature of man. . . . The regulation of these various and interfering interests forms the *principal* task of modern legislation.[9]

The question of course is whether there is not more to government than that; which means whether there is not more to man that that. Is the war won that easily—by *either* side? Or does the factionalism within us and between us somehow have to be held in tension with the community?

For those who are factious . . . there will be wrath and fury. (Rom. 2:8)

Where jealousy and selfish ambition exist there will be *dis*order and every vile practice. (Jas. 3:16)

Is there not something in churches moving church members to fulfill the demands of relationship, to establish community, to get for the other guy what they have already gotten for themselves, to give the other guy what was already been given them, to think of the other guy *first?*

Why is it always considered realistic to bet on man's badness, the way Madison did, rather than on his goodness, the way Paul did, and Jesus, and Isaiah? Indeed, is this not *precisely* the point of the Biblical definition of justice: that there is *more* to life than every man's ruggedly pursuing his own self-interest? *Jesus*, Paul said, was the way out of his war. And who was Jesus? Jesus was the man who lived out the realism of the *other* side of man's nature: namely, that a man *could* put another man first. Altruism is *just as much* sown into the nature of man as egoism. And justice bets on that.

IV

Three, justice is obligatory. It is not negotiable. "Seek justice," Isaiah said for God. It was not a suggestion, it was a command. "Love your neighbor," Jesus said. It was not a suggestion; he specifically called it a commandment. The commands had to be given because they were the only way man could be challenged to come over to his other side. It was so difficult to come over, it went so much against what we thought was human nature, that we had to be *ordered,* and if we were servants we *would* obey, individually *and* collectively—*every* conceivable way. We would love our neighbors as ourselves, which, when spelled out, meant we would seek justice, which in turn meant, paradoxically, that we would say Yes to ourselves. We would do what was in us to do and put the other guy *first.*

Now against that bet, of course, *is* ranged the realism of 50 million (sic) people killed in wars in this century alone.[10] Against it is ranged our insanity in Vietnam. Against it is ranged our inveterate factionalism, as Madison predicted, from those in high places down to the least of us pursuing exclusively his own self-interest.

Against it, too, is ranged our indescribable nonchalance about the very process of justice itself.

60 per cent of the eligible do not vote regularly; half of them cannot name their congressmen; 65 per cent cannot name both of their senators; 86 per cent are not able to identify *anything* their congressman has done; 96 per cent cannot identify *any* policy their congressman stands for.[11]

Against our achievement of justice is also ranged our own cynicism about ourselves.

97 per cent of us [according to the Harris Poll] want a decline in violence; but only 31 per cent expect to get it. 96 per cent want an end to all wars; but only 32 per cent expect to get it. 87 per cent do not want to get ahead at someone else's expense; but only 29 percent think that is possible.[12]

They are all 3–1 bets against the angels of our better nature.

Is there any hope that we *will* "seek justice"? Is there any hope that we *will* "love our neighbors"?

The Christian church says that there is. The church are those who, in spite of all that is ranged against them, *hear* the commands. To hear in the Hebrew *meant* to obey. They are those who will do *everything*—from bills to political party to corporate power plays—to fulfill the demands of relationship with their brothers. They will do *anything* for community.

They do it because they feel, inexplicably, that it has *been* done for them. In the obedient self-sacrifice of Christ they have learned what it means to be in relationship. They marvel that his highest praise was reserved *not* for those who acted for their own benefit, but rather for those who fed the hungry, gave water to the thirsty, and showed mercy to all.

They marvel, in other words, that the demands of relationship *were* fulfilled for them. They did not think of the other guy first; but they were thought of first. They did not seek justice; but justice was sought for them. They did not establish community; but they were drawn into fellowship.

Because it happened to them, they would make it happen. And when they failed, they would still hope. The Suffering Servant was proof that they were still in *relationship*. "I will not forget you," Isaiah reported. God *is* what gets us to think of the other guy, first.

6

The Church as a
Third Force in America

Something is wrong. The mood of the country is not good. Cambodia is invaded. Laos is invaded. Vietnam drags on. Students are killed by national guardsmen. Thousands march. Thousands do not march. We are divided. Our divisions are deep. Some say they may rend us for good.

Violence is up. Crime is up. Dope is up. The market is down. Business is down. Human relations are down.

Things were equally askew in the time of the prophets. There was war then. There was injustice then. There was civil strife then. Specifically, the politicians were getting in the way of the people. The businessmen were putting profit over justice. And individual citizens were either exploiting or being exploited.

The prophets' quarrel with their social order [writes an expert] was that it did not enshrine and sustain the human and social values integral to [their faith], but on the contrary destroyed them.[1]

Therefore the prophets condemned with passion theft, oppression, greed. Something was wrong with their country. Particularly, something was wrong with their country's power structure. Fat priests, rich women, venal judges, heartless creditors, greedy landowners—these were the ones with whom the prophets quarreled.

> The Lord enters into *judgment* with the
> elders and princes of his people:
> "It is *you* who have devoured the vineyard,

the spoil of the poor is in your houses.
What do you mean by crushing my people,
   by grinding the face of the poor?"
                              (Isa. 3:14–15)

Something was wrong. The country had slipped its mooring. It needed the prophets to call it back. It had to go to work at once to avert disaster.

Take the war. The problem was that the country had come to put a false reliance on its military might. It had come to think that might was right; that because it had the horses it had the principles; that because it had the allies it had the morals.

Woe to those who go down to Egypt for help
   and rely on horses,
who trust in chariots because they are many
   and in horsemen because they are very strong,
but do not look to the Holy One of Israel
   or consult the Lord!
                              (Isa. 31:1)

Take the economy. The problem was that a capitalist class had arisen in Israel and stratified the country. The rich got richer and the poor got poorer. Prices rose. It was an age of affluence for some and an age of poverty for many. The problem was that the some could not have cared less about the many. Profit beat justice.

Woe to those who lie upon beds of ivory,
   and stretch themselves upon their couches . . .
who drink wine in bowls,
   and anoint themselves with the finest oils,
but are not grieved over the ruin of Joseph!
                              (Amos 6:4,6)

Take the politicans. The problem was that they were in league with the affluent to crush the poor. Judges took bribes. The king refused to pay a just wage. Laws were for the benefit of the few at the expense of the many.

> *Woe* to those who decree iniquitous decrees,
>   and the writers who keep writing oppression,
> to turn aside the needy from justice
>   and to rob the poor of my people of their right! . . .
>   (Isa. 10:1–2)

Take the people themselves, all the people, but especially the establishment people. The reason for the war was pride. The reason for the poverty was pride. The reason for the injustice was pride.

> Have we not by our *own* strength taken
> Karnaim for ourselves?
>   (Amos 6:13)

> Ephraim has said, "Ah, but I am rich,
> *I* have gained wealth for *myself.*"
>   (Hos. 12:8)

> This is the exultant city . . .
> that said to herself,
>   "*I am* and there is *none* else."
>   (Zeph. 2:15)

> You will be like *God*. . . . (Gen. 3:5)

II

The church among others is responsible. We are the cause. We did it. It's our fault. We are all in it together. We are particularly in it if we belong to the establishment, if we are part of the power structure in our jobs or in our community.

We cannot pass the buck to the politicians and businessmen. We may want to, but we cannot. We are responsible. It was corporate responsibility for corporate problems in the ancient Jewish communities. It still is. The Judeo-Christian tradition is corporate even *before* it is personal. God chose a people before he chose a man.

The word "democracy" comes from the words for "power" and "people." In a democracy the power is with the people.

The buck can no more be passed in the American democracy than it could in the Jewish theocracy. "We the people of the United States. . . ."

The problem however is the failure of people in churches to assume responsibility. And it is a problem clearly foreshadowed in ancient Israel. The nation resisted for centuries the natural urge to have a king. Finally they could resist no longer and serious trouble began. It was not only that Saul and the others were less than ideal. It was that the people in the religious communities, now that they had their king, washed their hands of responsibility for their destinies just as Pilate washed his hands of Jesus.

This is the Achilles' heel of democracy, just as it is of autocracy. Namely, that we elect people to govern our destinies and then forget about those destinies ourselves. America is not a democracy, it is a republic. Republican government is representative government. The trouble with representative government is that it is left to the representatives. It may be the best government there is, but it is flawed, and the flaw is the people. The governed invariably leave the government to the governors.

It is the assumption of *responsibility* that the prophets were after. They were continually calling the people to assume responsibility for the state of their nation. It was in a wretched state, and it was in that state precisely because the establishment ruled and the people did not. More to the point, it was in that state because the establishment had blocked the rule of God by blocking the rule of justice.

There are at least two establishments in our country that are as powerful as they were in Israel. One is political and the other economic. No other establishment in the country has anywhere near the power of these two. The educational does not. The cultural does not. The scientific does not. The technological does not. "The business of America is business," Calvin Coolidge said. It is also politics.

But let us back up a step. Although it may appear that the

power is in the government and the corporation, there is some question about whether it is really there. It may be that politics and business are not really "where it's at" in America. The *people* are where it's at—*if* they will assume responsibility as well as elect it.

Consider the politician. He is there to do the will of the people. That is his job. A member of the Mafia could sit in the legislature and cast the right votes *so long as the people kept him casting the right votes.* The *people* are where the power is—*if* they will assume responsibility as well as elect it.

Consider the businessman. He is there to do the will of the people who own his company. That is *his* job. A member of the Mafia could sit on a board of directors and cast the right votes *so long as the shareholders kept him casting the right votes.* Admittedly this is difficult when shareholders' meetings last only twelve minutes. But the *people* are where the power is— *if* they will assume it as well as buy it.

In the light of their essentially theological view of Israel's history, the prophets hold that the nation is constituted *not* by its political struc-ture centered in the king, his judges and officials, his army and his laws; *nor* by the official cult with its priesthood; *nor* yet by its economic organization and institutions. *The nation is the people,* constituted as such by the covenant and characterized by the social ethic "written in" to the covenant.[2]

III

If, then, something is wrong with our country—and if each of us assumes responsibility for its being wrong—how are we to set it right?

It is time for the formation of a Third Force in America. It is time for a national uprising of the people to regain control of their destinies. It is time for a grassroots, populist movement which will bend the political and economic establishments to its will. And it is time that this movement be organized through the churches and synagogues of America.

The people are where the action is in this country, and the church is where the people are. No other institution touches so many American lives. Almost two-thirds of America belongs to church and synagogue: 130 million people. Two-thirds of every community belongs to that community's religious institutions. Two-thirds of every school board, two-thirds of every city council, two-thirds of every state legislature, two-thirds of every congress, two-thirds of every board of directors, two-thirds of every labor union are *already* in the churches. In many cases it is virtually 100 percent.

If something is wrong with the country, and if the key to righting that wrong is the people, surely one key to the people is galvanizing the one institution that is in touch with most of them. That is *precisely* what the prophets were trying to do. They were trying to get the people *through* their religious communities to *assume* the responsibility for God's justice which they had given up.

If politics and economics were enough, we would not be in the predicament we are in. They are patently not enough. The people have had to take to the streets precisely *because* they are not enough.

It is time to give the power back to the people. "We the people of the United States. . . ." That was the point of the American Revolution, and that is the point of this revolution. For the first time in history a country bet on the people. That was the American dream. And it came straight from (among other places) America's religious roots.

The *people* are where the power is in a democracy. The *church* is where the people are in this democracy. Therefore turn on the church to turn on the people to seek justice. That is how Isaiah put it to his people in his first chapter: "Seek justice."

The Third Force in America *are* the people. Most of the people belong to the churches and synagogues. Therefore the Third Force are the people in the churches and synagogues and elsewhere who can turn this country around for justice—*if* they will. Even if the church were pared to the bone, it would still be the Third Force, making up in quality what it lacked in quantity.

Justice, and only justice, you shall follow, that you may live and inherit the land which the Lord your God gives you. (Deut. 16:20)

The word for justice, as we have seen, meant case law. Case law meant to restore community. *Every church and synagogue in America is charged with working for laws that will restore community and bring the justice we have let only our politicians seek.*

It is objected that this is not the job of the church. The most the church can do is to tell people to get active in their political parties.

The objection is Biblically illiterate and historically naive.

> I hate, I despise your *feasts,*
>   and I take no delight in your *solemn assemblies.* . . .
> Take away from me the noise of your *songs;*
>   to the melody of your *harps* I will not listen.
> But let justice roll down like waters,
>   and righteousness like an everflowing stream.
>   (Amos 5:21, 23-24)

It is clearly the job of the church to seek justice. To be a church *is* to seek justice.

The injunction to do it through your political party would be fine if it were being done. But it is not being done. That is basically the reason for the malaise we are in. Even a progressive state can muster only 3 percent of the population for its precinct caucuses—the one massive attempt to induce the people to be political and take control of their own destinies.

It is objected that the Third Force would be a third political party. It is nothing of the sort. It is an attempt to organize the people to put the pressure on both political parties to approximate justice. "Justice, only justice, you shall follow."

The Third Force works *on* the present political and economic establishments to secure the justice our religious tradition *tells* us to secure.

The name of the game is to organize. That is the only way in which the will of the people can ever be felt. There is no use wringing our hands over Vietnam if we do not organize to prevent future Vietnams. If we *had* been organized, if the Third Force had been actual rather than potential; if, in other words, churches and synagogues had been *doing their jobs,* there might never have been a Vietnam war in the first place.

IV

How do we organize?

One, every church in America can take a vote every Sunday on the most burning issue before the country, state, or municipality, and that vote can be recorded with the appropriate congressmen, state legislators, and city councilmen. The Gallup Poll samples 1,600 people. There are 60 million people at worship every week. Let us take up the vote as well as the collection.

Two, every church in America can follow up its vote with action on those issues the people of the church feel are the most burning. By action I mean such things as inundating the offices of elected officials, coalescing with other groups, doing *whatever* may be necessary to achieve the justice the church and synagogue members are charged to seek.

Three, the churches of America can elect shadow governments from the local level up to the federal. This means a shadow mayor from the Third Force, a shadow city council, a shadow state representative and senator, and a shadow congressman and U.S. senator. The purpose of the shadow governments would be to get through loud and clear to the duly elected popular governments what the Third Force feels about such matters as war, pollution, the military-industrial complex, superhighways through living rooms, and so on. Presumably

this kind of thing could be done directly to the popular government. But that is the point. It has not been done. The minute
it is, regularly and forcefully, the shadow government can cease
to exist.

Four, every element of the Plan of Church Union of the nine
major American Protestant denominations which does not organize the new church along these or similar lines for social
action to achieve social justice can be scrapped.

Such sentences as the following are so anemic as to be virtually worthless in the 1970's:

Men and women of all ages are the church as they are involved in the
daily affairs and crises of industry, government, education, societal
relationships, cultural development, recreation, and family.

An action plan for the new church must be written fast. It
could be written by such men as sociologist Peter Berger, editor
Stephen Rose, ex-Catholic bishop James Shannon, and the committee could be chaired by such a man as Saul Alinsky, who is
a Jew and one of the best organizers in the country.

Where in this society [reads a college editorial] is there an institution,
that is an effective power within the structure of the society, that
exhibits an active concern for the humanness of man? Where?

And they shall beat their swords into plowshares,
   and their spears into pruning hooks;
nation shall not lift up sword against nation,
   neither shall they learn war any more. . . .
                                        (Mic. 4:3)

Church and synagogue are charged with keeping that vision
current and hot. They are charged with doing *everything* for
the humanness of man. Their *job* is to get justice. *Now.*

7

The Marks of a Successful Church

The success of any business can be measured. Either it makes money or it doesn't. By the same token, the success of any church can be measured. Either it makes Christians or it doesn't.

Admittedly, church success is more elusive than that of business. For one thing, it is easier to measure money than Christians. For another thing, it is impossible to succeed as a church. No matter how many Christians are made, it is never enough. No matter how much a church "succeeds," it never succeeds enough.

Nevertheless, a church's success *can* be measured. There are calipers. There are parameters. There are percentages. There are enough data for a quarterly report. It should appear in the local press. It should not be left to the imagination. It should not be left solely to the Holy Spirit.

I

One, a precise indicator of a church's success is how much of its money it gives away. Churches are in business to lose money. A church's profit is its loss. Jesus lost everything. "Whoever loses his life for my sake will find it." That is how Christians are made.

Now admittedly, money isn't everything. But it is something. In America in the 1970's it is a precise indicator of what Americans of the 1970's value. "Where your treasure is, there will your heart be also."

The sad fact of the matter is that most American Christians

value profit over loss. They would rather get than give. The average Protestant church gives 21 percent of its receipts away. "I was hungry and you gave me food." When it should be giving *at least* 51 percent. "I was thirsty and you gave me drink." That is why Christians are not being made in America in the 1970's.

Admittedly, the 79 percent they spend on themselves is being used by churches to make Christians more Christian. But the world is not going to wait around while we try to do that. Besides, the emphasis is wrong. What you get for yourself in Christianity is a *by-product* of what you give to others. "Sell what you have and give to the poor." One form of giving is institutional.

What other institution gives *more* than it gets? The church has a chance to *be* the servant its founder was. "I am among you as one who serves." It has a chance to show that it cares for others *more* than itself. "If anyone would come after me let him deny himself."

It isn't easy. Some would even argue it is against human nature. Jesus would argue that it *was* human nature. He would argue that we have not begun to explore what we are capable of becoming. At the very most, William James is reported to have said, we measure up to only 10 percent of potential. "With God," Jesus said, "all things are possible."

Eighty *billion* dollars' worth of real estate is owned by churches. [1] That is double the combined assets of America's five largest industrial corporations.[2] It is equal to the annual budget of the Department of Defense. Seven billion dollars a year are contributed to churches.[3] *At least* 51% should be given away.

The church could help do in the area of hunger, poverty, and the rest what the government cannot do alone. The church, through the power of the Suffering Servant, could help do what the government, through the power of the ballot and the bill, cannot do alone. Talk about reordering our national priorities: the church, if it became galvanized as a Third Force in American life, could do it.

II

Two, a precise indicator of a church's success is how many of its people it gives away. "I was sick and you visited me." It is a matter of giving more than money. It is a matter of giving self. "I was in prison and you came to me."

A Christian's job is to give himself away. Any church is in business to get its members to give themselves. "You shall love your neighbor as yourself." A church which does not move its members to give themselves away is not yet in business as a church.

Admittedly, it is hard to measure self-giving. But again, there *are* calipers. There are parameters. There are percentages. It is a dodge to say we cannot measure self-giving in churches.

How much money, for instance, does the individual church member give, as well as how much money does the church as an institution give? The percent of a man's income that he gives away is a precise indication of how serious he is about his religion, which *tells* him to give his money away. Jesus talked about money so much because he knew that giving money was a *precise* way to measure giving self.

The average Protestant gives $87.00 a year to his church.[4] Based on a tithe this would mean that the average Protestant makes $870.00 a year, which he doesn't; median family income is $9,750.[5] To portray it in all its raw selfishness: if every church member were suddenly placed on public relief and gave a tithe of his average *welfare* payment, the income of America's churches, UPI writer Louis Cassels discovered, would be 35 percent greater than it is now.[6]

How much money a church gets its members to give is a *precise* indicator of how successful it is as a church.

*   *   *

It is the same with time. How much time a church gets its members to give is a precise indicator of how successful it is as a church. Give time to what? To establishing community. "I was in prison and you came to me." To picking up those who are at the side of the road. "Go and do likewise." Do we do it?

There are two ways to answer that question. One is with our allotted time and one is with our discretionary time. A man allots a certain amount of time each week to his job and his home. A woman allots a certain amount of time each week to her home, and she may or may not have a job. The *amount* of allotted time spent on establishing community can be *measured*. If it cannot be measured, then the person is not yet in business as a Christian. If I do not know how selling stocks or doing dishes creates community, then I have either the wrong job or the wrong yardstick. The church are the people who measure their allotted time by how effective it is in creating community.

If, for instance, my allotted time is spent with a corporation, how effective have I been in using it to do, among other things, something about world community and stopping the war in Vietnam?

At the very least, have I, with my fellow Christian managers, gone to the president of my company and requested, during the next thirty days, four hours of company time for a teach-in on our national agony, presenting both sides as articulately and passionately as my ad agency presents my product?

You argue that this is not an appropriate way to spend your allotted time. I argue that is precisely an appropriate way, and that if more of our allotted time is not so spent, we will let the moral leadership of our nation go by default, which is precisely what we have been doing and precisely why we are in the mess we are in.

*

It is the same with our discretionary time. The success of our discretionary time is measured by its involvement in creating community. At the very least, am I active in my political party?

To be sure, some of this time needs to be spent—indeed, must be spent—in re–creating ourselves so that we can create community. Some of us go to the golf course. Some of us go to the lake. Some of us go to Key Biscayne.

But most of us probably have far more discretionary time than we think, and probably manage it far less capably than we admit. Most people, for instance, have two entire *days* off a week. That is a great deal of time. It is more than three *months* of vacation a year. Most people also work an eight-hour day. But a day has 24 hours. Deduct 7–8 for sleeping, 1½ for eating, time for travel, and you find that you not only work 40 hours a week, but you are *given* 30 to 40 hours a week. That's *more* free waking time during the week than you get on the weekends. It amounts to *another* two to three months of vacation a year.

How much time a church gets its members to give to loving others as well as themselves is a *precise* indicator of how successful it is as a church.

III

Three, a third measure of a church's success is how attractive it is to young people. Mark was a boy at the end of Jesus' life. Barnabas was his cousin. Timothy was a young man. Onesimus, the slave, was young. Paul was young: "They laid their garments at the feet of a young man named Saul." Jesus himself was relatively young.

It is rare for a church to muster more than one-third of its youth. It is even rarer for a church to be in touch with those who are not its youth and not any other church's youth. Where have all the young ones gone? They have gone to places where they see *more* self-giving than in the organization *founded* on self-giving. They have gone to people who will risk a great deal— for them, the way Stephen did for Paul. Stephen died for Paul. It must have affected him. Stephen did the Jesus thing for Paul. *Then* Paul became a Christian. But young people today do not see the church doing the Jesus thing for them or for anybody else.

They do not see the church as willing to risk. It gives away only a fifth of its income. Do you call that risk? Its members give only one-fiftieth of theirs. Do you call that risk? Their time is spent on petty socializing or petty bickering or petty service. Who's taking any risks—when the whole thing was founded on risk?

"Once," Emerson said, "we had wooden chalices and golden priests. Now we have golden chalices and wooden priests." He meant that the institution had ossified. It had become an end rather than a means. It had captured its own leaders. They had become sleek when they should have become indignant. They had been bought when they should never have sold out. The price was inertia. The institution would not budge. No one would risk a lot in order to move a little.

Why should that kind of organization be attractive to young people? It shouldn't. As a matter of fact, it shouldn't be attractive to anyone. It should repel rather than attract. And the young people tell us it does.

However, the church does offer a voice. It does offer people. It does offer meaning. What other institution offers people that young a vote? The government has gone to 18; the church goes to 14. What other institution offers people of all ages, together, at once? What other institution is so bold as to claim an ultimate meaning for its members?

How many young people a church attracts is a *precise* indicator of how successful it is as a church.

IV

Four, a fourth measure of a church's success is how controversial it is in its community. The whole thing began in controversy. Jesus was executed as an insurrectionist. He taught in controversy. He lived in controversy. He died in controversy.

The precise charge against him was that "he stirs up the people." "I have not come," he said, "to bring peace, but a sword."

As we have seen, Jesus would disrupt community if need be —even the intimate community of the family—for the sake of a higher community, with God. There are two sides to Jesus— this one and the other, "Come unto me all ye who labor and are heavy laden." Unfortunately, we remember the second and forget the first. We let Jesus comfort our troubles, it has been said. But we do not let him trouble our comforts.

It was no different for the early church. They were controversial. When they hit town they were either thrown in jail or thrown out of town. "These men," said a mob, "who have turned the world upside down have come here also." They were called outside agitators, instigators of rebellion. They were whipped. They were jailed. They were hunted. They were killed.

Five times I have received . . . the forty lashes less one. Three times I have been beaten with rods; once I was stoned. (2 Cor. 11:24–25)

The church has always had an uneasy relation with the culture in which it exists. It is a radical group following a radical leader, and it will do radical things. If it does not, then it is not the church.

The reason we have given up on the church, say the young, is that we don't see the church *doing* the radical things their leader did. Take love, for instance, on a large scale. The church is the caboose on virtually every major social issue. It is late on almost every opportunity to build community. It was late on civil rights. It was late on Vietnam. It has been late on hunger, late on pollution, late on birth control, late on folk music. That is why the church no longer cuts it with the young.

To be a church *is* to be controversial. It lead *is* to annoy. The leadership style of the church is to be two steps ahead, not one. The safety of the one step is left to the politician; the controversy of the two steps is the *job* of the church.

What about giving more than you get? That's turning a value

upside down. That's radical. That goes to the root of our nature. That's controversial. Hardly anyone wants to do it. And yet it must be done. It is a value which must pervade our society, or our society as we know it may be undone.

It is the mark of a successful church that it never lets up on trying to turn the world upside down. It never lets up on creating controversy. If it isn't criticized it isn't doing its job.

> In a world of fugitives
> The person taking the opposite direction
> Will appear to run away.[7]

How controversial it is in its community is a *precise* indicator of how successful it is as a church.

V

Five, a final measure of a successful church is how honest it is about style. Jesus was. He knew *what* he had to do. That's content. He also knew *how* to do it. That's style. *He* knew how *he* had to do it. No one else had put the Messiah and the Suffering Servant together. He did. It is perhaps the most brilliant example of style in history. And when his own friend, Peter, threatened to get in the way of his style, Jesus called him "Satan" to his face.

Jesus' style was suffering. So was the early church's. It is not that he avoided joy; that would have been masochistic. Indeed, one of the charges against him was that he loved a good time. Nor was it that the first church enjoyed controversy. They wanted to be loved as much as everyone else. It was that somehow these men and women, because of that man, saw that they would have to accept—indeed, would joyfully accept—whatever the consequences of self-giving might be. On the one hand those consequences were suffering, controversy, and even death. On the other, they turned the world upside down.

The question, the serious question, before the church in the

1970's is whether we will be honest enough about our faith to give enough to suffer, and then see—or not see—our suffering become for someone else new life. It is a question of whether each church will do what *it* has to do to give what *it* has to give to suffer what *it* has to suffer to create what *it* has to create.

One church's style cannot be another's. Each develops its own way of the cross. The unspeakable tragedy in our day is that the churches—all with the right content—do not have the style. Even the young, the poor, the black, the hippies, the communists will say the church has the content. But the content is belied by the style. The faith is belied by the work. The church will not suffer, if need be, for what it believes, It will build a temple, but it will not raise a cross.

Every church must do its own dying. Every church must set its face steadfastly toward its Jerusalem. Every church must label satanic everything that gets in the way of its self-giving. Because every church is charged with turning the world upside down. And its success is being measured by a cynical and broken community around it.

8

The Church in Business

Demetrius made silver shrines. He was also a leading businessman. He was a spokesman for those in his business and for those in related businesses.

At the moment he was speaking. He was defending his business against Paul, whose preaching threatened to put him out of business.

Men, you know that from this business we have our wealth. . . . And there is danger . . . that this trade of ours may come into disrepute. . . . (Acts 19:25,27)

In his defensiveness, Demetrius did at least three things which church members are all tempted to do. It may be that church members are particularly tempted to do them if they are in business.

I

First, he put too high a value on money. If it made money, it was right. If it did not make money, it was wrong. Paul was wrong because what Paul said was not good for business. Because of Paul, the business of selling model shrines as souvenirs to pilgrims coming to the temple at Ephesus was falling off.

A thing is right if it makes money. "Men, you know that from this business we have our wealth." Therefore our business is right. It is not to be changed. Whatever opposes it must be opposed.

Now this of course is an extreme position, and in the modern world of business there are few such obvious cases of right and wrong. But the Bible is insistent. It does not treat the money question lightly. Time and again it goes after the desire of every man and institution—including the church—to put too high a value on money.

It is one thing to make money. It is another thing to make too much money. It is one thing to profit. It is another thing to profiteer. It is one thing to place a high value on money. It is another thing to place too high a value on money. "This night your soul is required of you," Jesus describes God as saying to the man who all his life placed too high a value on his money.

Perhaps the question is one of degree. The Bible does not say "money is the root of all evil." It says "the *love* of money is the root of all evil" (1 Tim. 6:10). Placing a high value on money as essential for the basics of life is one thing. Placing too high a value on money is another.

General Eisenhower warned us about the "military-industrial complex." It was the most memorable thing he said in his presidency. It is a Demetrian issue.

During the 1950's [according to a study by the Brookings Institution] virtually all large military contracts . . . ultimately involved costs in excess of original contracted estimates of from 300–700%.[1]

In his book, *The Military-Industrial Complex*, Sidney Lens reports that:

The true wealth of the Pentagon is from 300 to 400 billion, or about six to eight times the annual after-tax profits of *all* American corporations.[2]

A study was made of defense firms doing three-fourths of their business with the Government and industrial firms of comparable size selling their wares on the commercial market. The former earned 17.5% on investment from 1962 to 1965, as against 10.6% for the latter.[3]

Profits in the Minuteman program, from 1958 to 1966, were 43%.[4]

North American Aviation earned 612% and 802% profit on its investment in two successive years.[5]

Again, the example is extreme. Profits are one thing, excess profits another. But what is not extreme is the propensity in all of us who have some to want more. And it is precisely that propensity against which the Bible warns so strongly.

Why? Because the Bible sees it as self-serving. The more I make the more *I* make.

Beware lest you say in your heart, "*My* power and the might of *my* hand have gotten me this wealth." (Deut. 8:17)

The direction of my life is wrong if I place too high a value on money. I vaunt my ability. I get defensive about my self-interest. I think more highly of myself than I ought to think, as Demetrius did.

II

Second, he put too low a value on people. This is not the way it has to be in business any more than putting too high a value on money is the way it has to be. But it is the way it can be, and if the shoe fits we should admit it. The church in business are the managers who ask whether the shoe fits.

Paul got in the way of Demetrius' business, so Demetrius got rid of Paul. His defensive speech stirred up a mob, they dragged the Christians into the arena, and after two hours of demonstrating they rode Paul out of town. The competition was eliminated. The end of profit justified the means of violence.

And that, whether we like it or not, is precisely the way much of the world sees America. They do not see us protecting the cause of freedom. They do not see us opposing the cause of Communism. They see us doing anything to anybody anywhere in the world to make money. If that means allying with dictators, then it means allying with dictators. If it means consorting with repressive regimes, then it means consorting with repressive regimes. If it means a deaf ear to the legitimate aspirations of the people, then it means a deaf ear—and forgetting the legitimate aspirations of another people in 1776. "It is a problem of markets," Dean Acheson said.[6] Not democracy, not freedom, not people, but markets.

Our investments abroad now equal 20 percent of our domestic production and 10 percent of the aggregate product of the non-Communist economies; and they exceed the product of all national markets except those of the United States and Russia.[7]

On the one hand, why not? Invest in another country, build it up, pay its people good wages, raise the standard of living. Fine if it happens. But does it happen? Or is the money remembered and are the people forgotten? Are we in there for what we can get substantially more than for what we can give?

Lens reports on American private investment in Guatemala. Now more than fifteen years after it went in, three-fourths of the people still live on what the UN considers a "below starvation level," three-fourths are illiterate, four-fifths are without adequate water and toilets, one-fifth of the children die before they reach the age of five.[8]

Demetrius could not stand the foreigner, Paul. When the foreigner did something to threaten his profit, Demetrius threw him out of town. Profits *over* people. Money *over* men. Product *over* person.

The modern corporation is not and cannot be expected to be a "responsible" institution in our society. For all the self-congratualtory handouts depicting the large firm as a "good citizen," the fact remains that a business enterprise exists purely and simply to make more profits —a large proportion of which it proceeds to pour back into itself.[9]

A business, the argument goes, takes care of its social obligations through its taxes and through its charitable contributions. It is unrealistic to expect it to do more.And it is not only unrealistic it is unfair. That is the job of the government.

But is it? For one thing either the taxes are not sufficient or they are not efficient. The job of meeting our social obligations in America is not being done. For another thing, business contributions to charity are negligible. Under federal law business is permitted to contribute up to 5 percent of its pretax profits. However, business averages only 1.2 percent, which is less than half what the individual American averages in *his* charitable contributions.[10]

What then is to be done? Either we make money and forget Paul, or we make money and remember Paul. Presumably the Christian manager chooses the latter. The church in business is bringing *people* up toward the level of profits as never before —not *to* the level of profits, perhaps, but *toward* it.

What we must do [writes the head of IBM] is assign a higher order of priority to the *national* interest in our business decisions.[11]

Since the corporation derives its legitimacy from the state through its articles of incorporation [writes the President of Owens Illinois], its *basic* purpose must be to *serve society* through the production of the material wealth required by society.[12]

The question, of course, is *how* this is to be done. And answering that question will require all the imagination the church in business has. Some argue that business can provide the answer alone. Its assets are formidable. According to the *Harvard Business Review*, General Motors, for instance, the world's largest corporation, took in revenues in 1966 that exceeded the annual gross national products of all but 13 of the free-world nations.[13] Our 50 largest companies have almost 3 times as many people working for them as our 50 states, and their combined sales are over 5 times greater than the taxes the states collect.[14]

More argue, however, that business cannot solve our social problems alone, and that business and government must do together what neither can do separately. Indeed, it is argued, government is essential to the solution because it alone is answerable to all the people, whereas business is answerable to only 30 million of them, its stockholders. It is up to the government, elected by the people, to determine the nation's priorities and then, with business, to meet them, offering business tax incentives, matching funds, and standards that all must meet, so that doing good will be profitable as well as desirable.

But who puts the pressure on the government and business to see that the good gets done? *That is the job of the church in business and the church as the Third Force in American life.* The church's *job* is to remind business and government, through the Christian manager and through Christian power, that people are *as* important as profits. Christian power means everything from voting stock proxies as churches to lobbying as churches for consumer protection.

> Hear this, you who trample upon the needy. . . .
> (Amos 8:4)

> Woe to those who lie upon beds of ivory. . . .
> but are not grieved over the ruin of Joseph!
> (Amos 6:4, 6)

> Do you think you are a king
> because you compete in cedar?
> Did not your father eat and drink
> and do justice and righteousness?
> *Then* it was well with him.
> He judged the cause of the poor and needy;
> then it was well.
> Is not *this* to know me? says the Lord.
> (Jer. 22:15-16)

Or, as a modern-day prophet who was also board chairman of the greatest business success of the decade put it, Sol Linowitz of Xerox:

[American business must start making] social goals *as central* to its decisions as economic goals.[15]

III

Third, Demetrius did the one thing that could not be done if a church is going to stand in the Judeo-Christian tradition. He relativized the absolute. He brought God down to his level. He used his religion. "This Paul," he said, is "saying that gods made with hands are not gods." Precisely. What Demetrius had done was to make a religion of his business. It was the most important thing in his life. It was his god. All values were subservient to economic values. All measurements of success were economic.

The danger which the Bible saw so clearly was not that church members would place too high a value on money or too low a value on people. We would do that, to be sure. But the real danger, of which these two were only symptoms, was that we would relativize the absolute, that we would make God less than God, that we would substitute our values for his.

The hard fact of the matter is that God, in the Judeo-Christian tradition, does *not* place a high value on money *except* as it is used to establish social justice. We may not like that. It may go against our grain. It may violate everything we ever learned in the so-called "Protestant ethic." But nevertheless it is there. You cannot justify the making of money for the sake of making money in the Bible. People are *more* important in the Bible than profits. You make profits to help people. The *job* of the church is to remind business of that. The economic *serves* the social. Profits are a means, not an end. The end is justice; the means are profits. The end is altruistic; the means are hedonistic. The end is to better mankind; the means are to better yourself.

But the end is the end. The Gross National Product is justice; the Gross National By-Product is the total output of goods and services. To do justice, not to make money, is to know the Lord. The *job* of the church is to remind business of that. The church *are* the managers and labor leaders who remind business and labor of that.

> They have become great and rich,
>   they have grown fat and sleek. . . .
>   They judge not with justice
> the cause of the fatherless, to make it prosper,
>   and they do not defend the rights of the needy.
> Shall I not punish them for these things? says the Lord,
>   and shall I not avenge myself
>   on a nation such as this?
>
> (Jer. 5:28-29)

It was no different in the New Testament. If anything it was more stringent. "No one can serve two masters," Jesus said. "You cannot serve God and property." It is the old word for slave. You cannot be a slave of your possessions. The one must beat the other, and in the Judeo-Christian tradition the service of God must beat the service of money, which is to say a church member's money must be used for the purposes of God rather than his God being used for the purposes of his money.

Demetrius used his religion to serve his business. He used his god to make a profit. He invoked his god to cloak his self-interest. It was not because he loved Artemis that he was opposing Paul. It was because he loved Demetrius.

That is the point the Bible is making. Not just that church members value money over people, which we do. But that we value self over God. It was the point of the first story and it was the point of the last.

You say, I am rich, I have prospered, and I need nothing. (Rev. 3:17)

When a man needs nothing he does not need God.

Not knowing that you are wretched, pitiable, *poor*, blind, and naked. (Rev. 3:1)

"How hard it will be," Jesus said, "for those who have riches to enter the kingdom of God!" Why? Because they of all people, be they individual, or a church as in Revelation, or a business, or a nation, are sorely tempted to relativize the absolute. And when they do that, according to the history that is in the Bible, there can only be disaster.

In today's world [writes management consultant Peter Drucker] . . . the ultimate commitment . . . of the executive may well become a central ethical issue.[16]

Yes.

9

The Church in Politics

One of William Howard Taft's favorite after-dinner stories concerned a man who was assigned the topic, "The Christian in Politics."

Well [said the President], this fellow rose at the invitation of the toastmaster, gazed out over the expectant audience, bowed and commenced. "Mr. Chairman, ladies and gentlemen. I was assigned the topic for tonight's dinner, 'The Christian in Politics.' I did a great deal of research on the subject. I turned over half-a-dozen libraries. And my conclusion is simply this. There ain't no such thing." Then he sat down.

Fortunately not everyone shares his view. There are many who say that religion and politics mix. Church and state do not. That is America's great contribution to history. But religion and politics do.

If a man's religion is not relevant to his politics, then it is not religion. It may be superstition or magic or philosophy, but it is not religion. A man's religion is his ultimate loyalty, and it goes with him into the voting booth as well as the church pew.

Religion and politics mix because—to a degree—they have the same ends. Both are working for the betterment of man. Christianity calls it the kingdom of God. True politics calls it the just society. Neither the pastor nor the politician thinks he will make it. But both live as if they could. It is this living *as if* that is the touchstone of their faith.

Christianity and politics also use—to a degree—the same means to achieve their end. They believe that changed men change society, so they both seek to change men. To that extent they are both revolutionary. The little girl was not far off the mark when she said that the Bible begins in Genesis and ends in Revolutions. The Christian is a changed man, "a new creation," as Paul put it. And the true politician is always trying to change the citizen by "establishing justice," as the Constitution put it.

So saying, let us demonstrate the premise that Christ can be in a smoke-filled room as well as in an incense-filled church, by looking first at the Bible, then at the church.

I

The Bible is shot through with politics. It is a political document from stem to stern. It speaks of kingdoms and powers. It tells of intrigue and election. Above all it tells of a God who would be God, who insists on his sovereignty, who brooks no other gods before him—not Israel, not the church, and not the United States or General Motors either.

God is the creator and sustainer of all things, including political things. God is the redeemer of all life, including political life. God is love, and he loves citizens as well as saints, politicians as well as pastors. And he expects men and women to love him back, and to love each other, too.

But, as we all know, not even the mythical first man made the grade, nor the first man's son. "Am I my brother's keeper?" Cain asked God after murdering Abel. "What have you done?" the Lord replied. "The voice of your brother's blood is crying to me from the ground." So the Lord kicked Cain out of the country, condemning him to wander forever. He made him into a bum, the political irresponsible par excellence.

Throughout the entire Old Testament the Lord and his people are concerned with political responsibility. The chosen people were citizens of God's country. They obeyed God's laws. They were made in his image. They were responsible for all their actions, political as well as pious, to him.

And whenever they forgot any of these facts they were spoken to by God's prophets. "Seek justice," Isaiah said in the perfect political motto. "Let justice roll down like waters," Amos said, "and righteousness like an everflowing stream."

But there was always a tension between the prophets, the political responsibles, and the people. The people never rang doorbells for the prophets' platforms. They wouldn't have elected Isaiah dog catcher, or camel catcher as it would no doubt have been.

So God, as James Weldon Johnson said in "God's Trombones," had to take his hat off the hook and come down here himself. God got in there, just the way the politician gets in there. He went to the courts and the churches and the prisons; he talked with the lepers and ate with the outcasts and visited the State Mental Health Hospital.

"Love your neighbor as yourself," he said. And he spelled it out carefully for them, so that everyone would know exactly what he meant. And that was what got him in trouble. Because whenever you spell love out—when you go far enough—you get into politics.

"Feed the hungry," he said—instead of watching the children in Biafra starve.

"Welcome the stranger"—instead of running him out of the neighborhood.

"Visit the sick"—instead of tolerating ghetto conditions that produce sickness.

"Go to the prisons"—instead of sending someone else in there for you.

And then he told them a story to bring it all home.

A man was on the Interstate when he stopped for some hitchhikers. They dragged him from behind the wheel, beat him up pretty badly, and left him by the side of the road.

Now by chance a pastor was going down that road; and when he saw the man he passed by on the other side. After all, you could be sued, you know.

So likewise an assistant pastor, when he came to the place and saw him, passed by on the other side. Being from a different part of the county, it was obviously none of his affair.

But a member of the Weatherman faction of the SDS coming by stopped his car, took a first-aid kit out of the glove compartment, and stanched the man's bleeding. Then he put him on the back seat of the car and rushed him to the emergency room of General Hospital. Later he told the business office to send him the bill.

Which of these men was socially responsible? Christ asked. Which was his brother's keeper? Which sought to better his brother's condition? The establishment lawyer he was talking to didn't like it, but he got the point.

Nobody else liked it much, either. So they took the man out and nailed him between two thieves at the side of the highway leading into town, and the state troopers shot craps at his feet.

II

We have the means; we lack the will. We have the brains; we lack the heart. We have the knowledge; we lack the drive.

Religion gives us the drive. It provides the heart. It creates the will. Religion in the Judeo-Christian tradition demands justice. It commands justice. It orders justice.

Justice costs. It means hard work. In a democracy it is the job of the *people* to define values. It is the job of the *politicians* to put those values into action.

It is the job of the *people* to define priorities. It is the job of the *politicians* to legislate ways to meet those priorities. The trouble in most communities—and cities and states—is that values are rarely defined and priorities almost never set.

It is the job of the *church* to give people values and set their priorities. It is the job of the *church* to keep the demands of justice before the conscience of society. It is the job of *politics* to meet, step by step, the demands. And it is the job of the *people* to keep the politicians meeting the demands.

Whenever religion flags, justice is cheap. Whenever politics flag, justice is dear. Whenever the people flag, justice is—never.

The church is one of the instruments of religion. If it is the job of a man's religion to give him his values and set his priorities, then the church—as a broker of religion—becomes not only important, but crucial. It is particularly crucial because, unlike Jesus' time, the people who *are* the church *hold* the power. They, we, are *responsible* for seeing that justice is done.

The church, to this extent, *leads* the state. Churches lead, legislatures catch up. Morals are first, laws catch up. Religion is first, politics catches up.

Conscience is first, economics second. Human rights first, property rights second. Human values first, economic values second.

"With public sentiment," Lincoln said, "nothing can fail; without it nothing can succeed. Consequently, he who moulds public opinion goes deeper than he who enacts statutes or pronounces decisions."

The church therefore has an obligation to speak when power is misused. It has an obligation to act when justice is not being sought by powerful men. Justice is the political equivalent of love. Power is the means of obtaining justice. Politics is the fight for power. And whenever power is gained viciously or used selfishly or corrupts men absolutely, then the church has no choice. It must lay the Christian conscience on the political line.

This means that Christians have no business moralizing in their churches while their cities rot. It means they have no business going their safe, antiseptic way while ghettos are spawned, education in them debased, and the worst war in the history of our country drags on. The Third Force must act.

Fortunately, Christians have a long history of getting in there and slugging it out for the things they believe. Christianity is a roll-up-your-sleeves religion. It abounds in stormy petrels and revolutionaries who are impatient to push society ahead a little in the name of their Lord.

They are appalled by *Redbook*'s report of the survey of 4,000 Protestant pastors which concluded that:

Ministers today do not feel free to express their views on controversial subjects. . . . 1 out of 5 got into trouble after championing some social action program. . . . 1 out of 3 was scored by parishioners after including controversial subjects in sermons.

Shirtsleeve Christians do not wince at laying their religion on the political line. They never hide by saying their religion is their "private affair." It isn't. There is no such thing as "private" religion. To say that your religion is your private affair is to say that it means so little to you that you are not willing to stand up and be counted for it. Nothing worthy of the name religion ever meant so little.

Christianity is what it is today because yesterday the good news about Jesus got around. It got around because church members were not afraid to talk about Christ's lordship of all life, including political life. *"Kyrios Christos,"* they said in the political arenas. "Christ is Lord." And then they, too, were murdered.

The shirtsleeve Christian never views politics as too dirty to be in. It is no dirtier than the ministry, he says. It is silly to talk about being "above politics." It is foolish to use the word "politics" as a pejorative. It is hypocritical to run for office by trying not to look like a politician, whatever that looks like.

It is crucial, then, that the church member never fancy himself too good for politics. Politics is the same as the rest of life, only rubbed a little rawer, perhaps. There is self-interest and compromise and fighting. But these are in the church, too, and throughout life. The important thing is to channel this self-interest and compromise and fighting into laws for the betterment of man. And the key to that is to make politics ethical, to make it "one's own doing," which is what the word "ethics" means at its root.

Communist politics are tyrannous precisely because they are

not tempered by religion. "There is no morality in politics," Lenin said, "only expedience."

And much religion is sentimental nonsense precisely because Christians look the other way when it comes to political issues. They looked the other way in Cuba under Batista, and they got a Castro. They looked the other way in Germany under Hitler, and they got an Eichmann.

Religion and politics mix, and religion and politics had better mix or we're in for some tough times indeed.

"Seek justice," Isaiah said. "Love thy neighbor," Christ said. Let us take our stand beside them in the smoke-filled rooms.

10

The Church and Money

I

American church giving is an insult to Christ. It is brazen to call ourselves Christians and give so pitifully to Christ's work through the church. As we have seen:

The average American Protestant gives his church $87.00 a year.[1] That's less than $1.68 a week. It's less than 24 cents a day.

Of that amount, the average American Protestant gift to church-related benevolences is $18.41. That's 35 cents a week. It's 5 cents a day.

Of *that* amount, the average American Protestant gift to foreign missions was $2.95 in 1965.[2] That's a nickel a week. That's not even a penny a day.

In other words, the average Protestant is so enchanted with his religion that he is willing to sacrifice the equivalent of a can of frozen orange juice a day for it. He is so stunned by the claims of Christ on his life that he is willing, as we have seen, to give up the equivalent of a hog dog a *week* at a ball park to feed the hungry and clothe the naked and care for the sick (Matt. 25:35). And he is so taken with Christ's commission to the church to "Go . . . and make disciples of all nations" (Matt. 28:19) that he gives the equivalent of a pack of Life Savers a *week* to getting the good news around the world.

Now admittedly, averages are averages. They can mislead. For one thing, there are many Protestant church members who are only 14 years old. Eighty-seven dollars for a 14-year-old is unheard-of.

For another thing, there are obviously a great many Protestants who give sacrificially.

For still another thing, most families make only one "pledge" for husband and wife. The averages deal with individuals, not families. Thus what is $87 for a church *member* could be $174 for a church *family*.

Nevertheless, the averages, as in many statistical compilations, are the best thing with which we have to work. And the averages are not flattering.

Nor are the totals. *Protestant* giving in 1969 totaled $3.1 billion. That looks like a lot. It isn't.

It was less than half of 1 percent of the gross national product.

It was less than the net *profits* of our three largest corporations.

It is helpful in this regard to remember the rich man who came to Christ (Mark 10:17–22). He had everything going for him, as many church members have. He ran to Jesus, which suggests enthusiasm. He knelt before him, which suggests reverence. He kept the commandments, which suggests he was basically good. On top of all this he was rich.

But when Jesus told him his price—"Sell what you have, and give to the poor"—the man would not meet it. "His countenance fell, and he went away sorrowful." He was unable to fulfill a *condition* of church membership. He would not sacrifice. In other words, no sacrifice—no join. The rich man at least had the honesty not to join an organization whose standards he refused to meet.

We too are rich, many of us, and I daresay we are basically enthusiastic, reverent, and good. But for the moment let's concentrate on our richness—or "affluence," to use the cliché. Oh, I know we joke about it and say we can hardly make ends meet, and that we're not quite sure where the next payment is coming from, and that we haven't eaten steak or been to a movie in six months, and that we haven't bought a new suit in six years, and that inflation is eating up all our hard-earned cash, and that Uncle Sam is siphoning most of it off in taxes, and that what Uncle Sam doesn't get the school board does. Maybe we say all these things because deep down we're a trifle embarrassed, or defensive, or maybe just a little self-conscious about all the money we really do have.

If your family income is over $7,000 a year, the Census shows, you are in the top 63 percent in America. If you make over $10,000 a year you are in the top 39 percent. If you make over $15,000 a year you are in the top 15 percent. This means of course that, since America is the richest nation, many American church members are among the richest people in the *world.*

To see this a little more graphically, perhaps it is helpful to remember that

America is the first place on earth where people spend more on *wants* than on needs.[3]

America is the first nation in history to have *more* of its people employed in providing services than in making goods.[4]

Our economy is growing at a rate which will *double* in the next twenty years. This means there will be as much growth between 1965 and 1985 as between the *Pilgrims'* time and 1965.[5]

* * *

All right, if we have all this money, what are we going to do with it? That's a moral question, a religious one. It is a question about values, about priorities. If we belong to the church our values and priorities are *set.* We are *not* "perfectly free to spend our money any way we like." "Take up your cross," Jesus said. "I was hungry, and you gave me food, I was thirsty and you gave me drink" (Matt. 25:35). *Church members use their affluence to relieve other people's suffering.*

Item. 10,000 people die every day from starvation and malnutrition. (Louis Cassels)

Item. There are 17,000,000 refugees in the world. (U.S. Committee for Refugees)

Item. The 1970 Peru earthquake killed 50,000 people. The Pakistan cyclone 150,000.

Right here in America, according to the Census:

25 million live in poverty.

One-seventh of all American children live in poverty.

One-seventh of those 25 and over have less than an eighth-grade education.

One-eleventh of Americans do not live in decent housing.

The *only* standard for Christian giving is *sacrifice*. And one of the best standards for sacrifice, as suggested before, is the *tithe*. "Of all that thou givest me I will give the tenth to thee," Jacob said (Gen. 28:22).

Now, admittedly, he said it, or is reported to have said it, 3,600 years ago. And, admittedly, taxes on affluent people then were not the same as they are on affluent people now. They may well have been more.

The point is that discipleship costs, and if it does not cost it is not discipleship.

It may be objected that the tithe is too much for the little guy. That may be. But many American church members are not little guys.

It may be objected that we are already giving as much as most people do. "What do ye *more* than others?" Christ asked (Matt. 5:47).

It may be objected that we won't have enough for a rainy day. But our insurance programs and our savings programs are taking care of that.

It may be objected that we are already giving through our taxes. So was the rich man who came to Christ. Taxes are neither voluntary nor are they adequate. How many cancer funds and heart funds and United Funds and church funds are financed by taxes?

It is presumptuous, to say the least, for affluent American church members to pontificate about world poverty when they are not giving away at least 10 percent of their incomes to creative Christian ways of overcoming it. And it is naive, to say the least, for affluent church members to decry the spread of communism around the world when they are so entranced by its greatest competitor, Christianity, that they give to Christianity's foreign missions the grand average of *five cents a week*.

If a church member is not willing to pay the price, then there is no point in his being a church member.

II

Jesus knew that you could talk about love and God and things like that forever, but that not until you got specific about those things by putting a price on them would you ever begin to *change* the direction of a man's thinking from himself to God. Twenty, therefore, of his thirty parables had to do with money.

One of them told about a church member who had a lot of money and another who had none (Luke 16:19–31). The other was sick and poor. He was so poor that he ate what was in the rich man's garbage can, and he was so sick that he could not ward off the dogs in the street who came to lick his sores.

Unfortunately the rich man did nothing for the poor man. Ultimately they both died, and in the afterlife their fortunes were reversed, with the rich man in hell and the poor man in heaven. By then it was, of course, a trifle late to do anything about the poor man's suffering on earth.

What is the point? That the rich church member was selfish. And more. If you are going to be selfish about your money, Jesus is saying to church members, then you can take your money and go to hell with it. That is precisely what he is saying. If you are going to be selfish about your money, then you can go to hell.

Now that, of course, is a very serious thing to be saying. But Jesus was not only canny; he was tough. "The kingdom of God is preached," he said only three sentences earlier, "and every one enters it violently." He didn't mince. He didn't pussyfoot. He called a spade a spade. And, as perhaps nowhere else, Jesus got tough in his talk about money. Why? Because he knew that if he had the money he had the man.

III

It is an old principle, and a good one, that we can often act ourselves into a new way of thinking more readily than we can think ourselves into a new way of acting. That is to say, if a church member *gives* his money he will *change* his thinking. But if he waits around to change his thinking he will by no means necessarily give his money.

A church member is canny, and he knows the rut into which his thinking processes can get him. He knows that he often needs something to jar him out of the rut. What he needs is to act. Hamlet is one of literature's prime examples of thinking men. But Shakespeare summed up the flaw in Hamlet's character when he wrote, "Thinking too precisely on th' event," he failed to *act.*

If we sit around and look profound in our *koinonia* groups, thinking about how we are going to get from self-centered to other- and God-centered living, the chances are we are never going to get there. If, on the other hand, we act instead of think, do instead of stew, and give our money to poor and sick people, the chances are, Jesus is saying, that we will pass from self-centered to other- and God-centered living.

The church member's advantage is that he knows this. This does not mean, of course, that he will do it, but it does mean that he knows it. If he knows it, it is at least conceivable that he will do it. On the one hand, Jesus was optimistic. He had the rich man in hell ask Abraham in heaven: send the poor man back to earth to tell my five brothers what I learned too late. "If someone goes to them from the dead," the rich man said, "they will repent"—that is, change their minds, which is what the word repent literally means.

But Abraham refused to do it. They have "Moses and the prophets," he said, which meant that they had all the means at their disposal to do what they knew they should do. And that was the source of Jesus' optimism. They had the scriptures, they had the laws, they had the commandments. Sending someone back from the dead isn't going to help, Jesus was saying. You have all the evidence you need. Now all you need is to get going. All you need is to *act*.

On the other hand, Jesus was pessimistic. He was by no means sure that a church member, even with the equipment he had, would give his money away. That is why he was so tough in his language. That is why he talked about money so often. That is why when the epitome of the affluent American church member, the rich man, came before him, he didn't waste his time talking to him. He didn't suggest that he join a *koinonia* group and kick his problem around. He gave him his *orders*. "Sell what you have," he said, "and give to the poor."

Somewhere along the line we got hold of the idea that we are not under orders in our religion. "Go," Christ said, "and make disciples of all nations." But we take it or leave it. "Give to the poor," he said. But we say, "I have three children, the mortgage, and college." "Go and do likewise," he said about justice. But we don't.

Why will the church member accept orders in his business when he will not accept them in his religion? Why will he accept them in the military when he will not accept them in the church? Why will he even go so far as to order *himself* to do this and that in his business and family and not order himself to do comparable things in his religion?

IV

How much do church members give? In the Old Testament it was 10 percent. In the New it was more. "Sell what you have and give to the poor." Church members begin at 10 percent and work up.

Now there is nothing magical about the tithe. It is simply a guide, not a goal; a beginning, not an end. But it is an excellent guide and an excellent beginning. It is Biblical. And it begins, at least, to be sacrificial. Nobody pretends that a tithe on top of taxes and college and the mortgage and everything else is going to be easy. But that's all right. Church members are not challenged by what is easy. They are challenged by what is tough. They like to take the small company and make it big. They like to take the big company and make it bigger. They like to give enormous chunks of themselves—ten, twelve, fifteen hours a day—to the challenge of their jobs.

Two dollars a week for every thousand dollars of income. That's what the tithe works out to. If you are making $10,000 a year, that means $20 a week. It seems like a lot of money? It is. You're not giving that much? Give it. Our *orders* as Christians are to give sacrificially to poor and sick people. Which means that our giving to our churches' annual funds and benevolent funds plus all our other charitable giving should come to at least two dollars a week for every thousand dollars of income. "Of all that I have," Jacob said, "I will give the tenth to thee."

If we are not doing at *least* that much in the face of the world's suffering, then we are not being serious as Christians. If we are not doing at *least* that much, then, frankly, I am not even sure that I am a Christian at all.

It is late in the day to be hearing rich families cry poor when they should be helping the poor. It is late in the day to hear church members say, "I'll tithe, but not now." When is "now" ever going to come? There will be as many excuses at 50 as there are at 20, for old fathers as for young fathers. We have our obligations throughout life, and what Christ is arguing in this parable is that one of those obligations be the poor and the sick.

What about "now" for the children who are starving? What about "now" for the retarded children? What about "now" for the Arab refugees in the middle of the desert with no shelter, literally nothing over their heads? When a church member, living in a $30,000 house, says that he cannot afford to give sacrificially to put milk in the mouths of babies and roofs over the heads of families in deserts, then there is no question what Christ is saying to that man in this parable. He is saying: "Rich man, take your money and go to hell with it."

Two dollars a week for every thousand dollars of income. Let's quit the talking and start the tithing. Let's quit the excuses at which church members are so adept, and start the action, at which we sometimes balk.

Two dollars a week for every thousand dollars of income. If the time is not now, when is it? If we are not the ones to do it, who is?

11

The Church and Peace Within

It has always been a source of amazement where the early church got its strength. In spite of the most incredible adversity, it was able to carry on. Indeed, it not only carried on, it flourished. How can we have the same strength?

There are many answers to such a complex question, but surely one of them is in the book of Acts: "They devoted themselves to the apostles' teaching and fellowship, to the breaking of bread *and the prayers*" (2:42).

The early church was a praying church. The movement out was balanced by the movement in. The giving was balanced by the receiving, the servanthood by the childhood, the acting by the waiting, the talking by the listening, the emptying by the filling.

It is this balance which characterizes not only the religious but the human life. Churches get out of whack when they are all action and no prayer or when they are all prayer and no action. To be human is to pray as well as to preach. It is to seek peace within as well as between. Let's root those assertions in the human condition.

I

First, we are at war. That is the place to begin. Every man is divided against himself. The early church was no exception. Paul was its chief antagonist. Peter denied Jesus. Judas betrayed him. The disciples left him. They were torn about what to do after he died. As we have seen Paul wrote:

I find it to be a law that when I want to do right, evil lies close at hand. For I delight in the law of God, in my inmost self, but I see in my members another law *at war* with the law of my mind and making me captive to the law of sin. . . . (Rom. 1:22–23)

Jesus himself was at war. He was a man. He went into the wilderness in search of himself. He prayed, Luke says, "until his sweat became like great drops of blood falling down upon the ground" (22:44). And at the end he said, "My God, my God, why hast thou forsaken me?" (Mark 15:34).

But it goes back beyond Jesus. "Thou hast deceived me," Jeremiah said as he prayed (20:7). Jacob wrestled all night with the angel of his better nature. Adam and Eve hid. Moses fought.

Prayer begins in struggle. Consider the struggle a man has with himself to pray at all. It is not easy. It is not natural. But it is human. Prayer *is* honesty about the division between who we are and who we might become. That is not all prayer is. But prayer is at least that.

II

Second, prayer brings peace. It may start with war but its point is peace. And when you have that kind of peace within, you can go out, as the first church did, and "turn the world upside down." How does the peace come?

For *one* thing, they prayed often. "Pray constantly," Paul wrote (1 Thess. 5:17). And they did. They prayed for each other. They prayed for strangers. They prayed for the sick. They prayed for the dead. They prayed for prisoners. They prayed for themselves.

"Everything," we are told by an expert in the Judeo-Christian tradition, is appropriate for prayer.[1] "Anything important to the believer may be the object of petition."[2] "Even the most trivial things are worthy of prayer, since everything is of importance in this human life which belongs wholly to God."[3] Perhaps that is why the Lord's Prayer contains only petitions.

Not only was anything appropriate, any time was appropriate. Morning and evening were the usual times. Or it might have been all day or three times a day or forty days. Night was a favorite time with Jesus. The only requirement was frequency. And he told the story of the widow who came back and back and back to secure justice from the judge. "Ask," he said, "and it will be given you. Seek, and you will find. Knock, and it will be opened to you" (Luke 11:9).

Nor were there any word requirements beyond simplicity and brevity. "Do not heap up empty phrases," he said (Matt. 6:7). And then he gave them the Lord's Prayer, which is a model of simplicity and brevity. "Jesus," we are told by a scholar, "condemns the theory that if fifteen minutes of prayer is good, a half hour is twice as good."[4]

As a matter of fact, there need not be any words at all. Words were usual, but they were not necessary.[5] God responds to the weeping of a child as though it were a prayer (Gen. 21:16). He responds to Abraham as he is about to kill Isaac (Gen. 22:11). He responds to Hannah who "was speaking in her heart; only her lips moved; and her voice was not heard" (1 Sam. 1:13). He responds to the condition of the poor and the needy as itself a prayer (Isa. 41:17). "We do not know how to pray as we ought," says Paul, "but the Spirit himself intercedes for us with sighs too deep for words" (Rom. 8:26).

*

For *another* thing, they prayed everywhere. Any time. Anything. Any place. They prayed in the temple. They prayed in the upper room. They prayed at home. They prayed at meals. They prayed in jail. They prayed on the housetops. They prayed alone. They prayed together. They prayed in public. They prayed in private.

Again there are "no rules."[6] Anything. Any time. Anywhere. Any posture. It is particularly to be stressed that prayer was

A-6318

public as well as private. Corporate as well as personal prayer has always been deep within the Judeo-Christian tradition. That was the point of the disciples' request to be taught how to pray. Jesus' response was the Lord's Prayer. It is a group prayer.

Nevertheless, the profoundest moments of prayer were in solitude. "Religion," said Alfred North Whitehead, "is what the individual does with his own solitariness."[7] And in the Bible he does a lot. "He withdrew to the wilderness and prayed," Luke reports of Jesus (5:16). "And in the morning, a great while before day, he rose and went out to a lonely place, and there he prayed" (Mark 1:35). "He said to them . . . 'Remain here'. . . . And going a little farther, he fell on the ground and prayed . . ." (Mark 14:35).

Anything. Any time. Anywhere. But especially alone. Moses, forty days on the mountain, alone. Jesus, forty days in the wilderness, alone. Moses, alone at the burning bush. Jesus, alone on the hills. Elijah, alone in a far country. Jeremiah alone. Isaiah alone. Amos alone. Hosea alone. The Baptist alone. Stephen alone. Paul alone. "I went away into Arabia" (Gal. 1:17).

It is in solitude that a man confronts himself. It is in solitude that he hears his war. It is in solitude that he struggles to be the man he was meant to become. The church are the people who stand by each other in their solitudes.

Anything. Any time. Anywhere. But something. Sometime. Somewhere. In order to be himself, a man must confront himself. The church are the people who confront themselves. But there is more. Anyone can do that. Anyone can struggle to be what he was meant to be. The church are the people who try to be themselves by *denying* themselves.

III

That is the *third* thing to be said about prayer—that it brings peace in a particular way. It is the way of the cross. It is the way of defeat. The war is won by being lost. The church are the defeated. They are the conquered. "To him who conquers," said the Revelation writer, "I will grant to eat of the tree of life" (2:7).

Something. Sometime. Somewhere. The earliest gospel says that Jesus prayed at the great crisis moments of his life: before announcing his preaching tour, after feeding the multitude, before his arrest, on the cross.[8] It does not say that he prayed at his baptism. Nor at his transfiguration. Nor to heal. Nor to exorcise demons. Nor to raise the dead. What is the point? That he was confronting himself. A crisis is a time when a man in his solitude confronts himself. Will he conquer or be conquered? Will he win or be won? Will he go with himself or with God? Will he be a partial or a whole man?

Abba, Father, all things are possible to thee; remove this cup from me; *yet* not what I will, but what thou wilt. (Mark 14:36)

Jesus was whole because he allowed himself to be beaten. He allowed himself to be used. He won by losing. He became a *man* by including *God.* God *was* what used him. God *was* what defeated him. Prayer was the battleground. Peace was the result. And it was symbolized by the greatest peace symbol of all time, the resurrection.

The trouble with the church in the seventies is that it rarely prays. It is rarely used. It is rarely beaten. Where are the symbols of the church's being used? Where is the agony? Where is the peace? Where is the *humanity?* We have settled for partial rather than full life. The *only* thing the church has to offer is that it won't let a man be satisfied with partial rather than full life. It won't let him be less than a man. It won't let him be less than human. It won't let him buy a cheap peace. But where is the church *doing* that?

The word for prayer in the Old Testament came from the root for slashing oneself as an act of worship.[9] That is how far it goes back into our common humanity. From earliest times man realized that to be himself he had to give himself. God *was* what he gave himself to and *thereby* became a man. The symbol was the cutting, the radical self-denial that *meant* self-fulfill-ment. "If any man would come after me," Jesus said, "let him deny himself" (Mark 8:34). And then in the next sentence: "Whoever loses his life for my sake and the gospel's will save it." In his own prayer: "Not what I will, but what thou wilt."

That is the point of prayer. "Not what *I* will, but what *thou* wilt." The point is obedience. The point is surrender. The point is usefulness. The point is humility. The point is humanity. It is *not* self-transcendence. It *is* self-fulfillment. We are not *more* than men when we pray. We are *men*. The word for peace in the Old Testament came from the root for wholeness. When we pray we are on our way to becoming whole. That is why we experience peace when we pray. Time after time you "feel better" when you pray. The reason is that you have become more of a man. Not more *than* a man but more *of* a man.

Jesus was a *man*. He was more of a man than we will ever be, to be sure, but it is his manliness that encourages us to be men. Prayer is manly. It is human. It may not be natural. But it is human. The church are the people, at least in theory, who are trying to recover their humanity. The *only* thing a church has to offer is people who will stand by you in your solitudes as you struggle to be human.

But that's a lot. It was so much that the first church "turned the world upside down." It was so much that, inexplicably, they all felt their prayers were *answered*. *"Whatever* you ask in prayer," Jesus said, "believe that you receive it, and you *will"* (Mark 11:24). "The distinctive feature of early Christian prayer," writes an expert, "is the *certainty* of being heard."[10]

Of course. If the point of prayer is self-surrender, every time a person prays he is being honest about his need for help. He is *not* self-sufficient. If he were he would not be praying. Even prayers of thanksgiving imply surrender. You *need* the other to share your good news. God *is* what we ask for what we need. God *is* what we thank for what we have. God *is* prayer. "The Spirit *himself* intercedes for us." That is not all God is. But God is at least that. To pray *is* to be involved in the processes of God.

And to that extent prayers are always answered. The pray-er is, with every prayer, struggling to include God in his life and thereby experience the momentary peace of being a whole man.

Yes, there is an assumption, and the assumption is that wholeness includes Godness. For many that is obviously not true. But the question is, is it true for you, for me? The question every man has to ask, in the depths of his solitude, is whether he is *more* of a man with God or without.

The amazing thing is that the first church felt it *was* true for them. And with that fullness, that wholeness, that peace, they went out and turned the world upside down. They did all sorts of useful things. They even died at peace, which is the final test in our final solitude.

But that is not all. They went even farther. It is the most amazing thing of all. Their wholeness was such that they included not only God but the very ones who denied God. "Love your enemies," the man had said. "Pray for those who persecute you" (Matt. 6:44). And they *did*.

"Lord," Stephen *prayed* as he was stoned to death, "do not hold this sin against them" (Acts 7:60). It was the ultimate in the conquest of self. It was the ultimate in self-fulfillment. In wholeness. In humanity. In peace. It could only *be* God.

And as a man goes into the depths of his solitude to ask whether he is more of a man with God or without, he must contend with that.

12

Why Join the Church?

For many the church is not a live option. It makes no difference. It does not matter. It is not where the action is. It "does its thing" in its bourgeois ghetto. There is no reason to join. If you have joined, there is no reason to stay.

A person joins the Rotary Club for fellowship. He joins the country club for fun. He joins the political party for power. He joins the Y for athletics. He joins the firm for money. He joins the family for love. He does not see why he should join the church. If he has joined, he does not see why he should stay.

There is only one reason to join the church. For that matter, there is only one reason to join anything. You join it because it has something or does something you don't get anywhere else. What do you get in the church?

I

First, you get yourself. You join because it is in your self-interest. You will learn more about yourself by joining. You will experience more. You will be more effective as a person. "I came," Jesus said, "that you may have life, and have it abundantly" (John 10:10).

It was the Greek word for "surplus." It was the word for "superabundance." I join the church because I want my life to be superabundant. I want to experience everything I possibly am before I die. I want to think all there is to think. I want to feel all there is to feel. I want to do all there is to do. In a word, I want to maximize myself. I want to *be* myself; I want to be

105

everything it is in me to be. "I came that you may have life, and have it abundantly."

Now this, of course, is a curious place to begin—with myself and what I can get out of the church rather than what I can give to it. But maybe it is an honest place to begin. We join a thing for what we can get out of it. If we aren't getting anything out of it, we do not join. If we have joined, then we either get something out of it or we get out.

Consider the word for salvation. It meant to make whole. Jesus was offering a person wholeness. He was offering *every* person wholeness. "I came that you may have life," reads one translation, "and have it to the full." Jesus was offering full, whole, abundant, superabundant life. And the extraordinary thing is that he was offering it to *everyone*.

That was what was new. Surely the Jews offered abundant life, but they were offering it only to Jews. Jesus, a Jew, was offering it to everyone. Give up partial living, he was saying, for total. Sin is stopping. It is not going all the way as a man. It is not being what you were meant to be, thinking what you were meant to think, feeling what you were meant to feel, doing what you were meant to do. Salvation is wholeness. It is abundant life.

But why the *church?* I join the Rotary Club to make my life more abundant through fellowship. I join the country club to make my life more abundant through fun. I join the political party to make my life more abundant through power. And so on. Why the *church?* What is it the *church* offers that I don't get anywhere else?

A Man. You can talk all you want about organization. You can talk all you want about creed. You can talk all you want about faith and works and everything else. The fact of the matter is that what the church offers that you don't get anywhere else is a Man.

But can't you have the Man without the church? Yes. Then why the church? Because without the church you are less likely to have the Man. How do you know? I know myself. What does that mean? It means that without the church I would be less likely to take the Man seriously. The church are the people who take the Man seriously.

But can't you have abundant life without the Man? Yes. Then why the Man? Because without the Man you are less likely to have abundant life. How do you know? I know myself. What does that mean? It means that without the Man I would be less likely to want abundant life.

But the Man is gone. True. Then how can you have the Man? Through men.

II

That's the *second* thing I get in the church that I don't get anywhere else. I get other people. But you get them in the Rotary Club. You have just said you join the Rotary Club for fellowship. True. Then how can you say you get people in the church in a way you don't get them anywhere else?

That's just the point. I do get people in the church in a way I don't get them anywhere else. How? In what way? In the way that I am *for* them as well as for myself. To be myself I have to be for others. To be myself *is* to be for others.

But that's just common sense. It's simple psychology. The healthy self is the self that includes other people. Any psychiatrist or mother or father or youth—anybody—will tell you that. What does the *church* have to do with it?

Maybe the church is where I *practice* being for others as well as for myself. Maybe the church are the people who *keep me at* being for others as well as for self.

But don't they do that in the Rotary Club? They even wear badges which read "Service above Self."

OK. But how *much* service? A luncheon, a speaker, a scholarship, and that's about it for most Rotary Clubs. Maybe two scholarships.

A local church puts $5,000 into a laboratory school for dropouts; $9,000 into a street school for delinquents; $13,000 into scholarships for Indians. Maybe the church does *more*. The way the Man did. 'If any man would come after me, let him deny himself." The church are the people who remind each other of things like that.

But can't you be reminded without the church?

Yes. But *will* I be? Will I be challenged to put that kind of thing into action apart from the church, or will I be like most people and not even *hear* that kind of thing apart from the church—because (*a*) I won't *read* it, and (*b*) I won't hear anybody else but the church *saying* it?

Furthermore, even if I were to hear it myself and do it, is it not *more* effective to do it together rather than alone? Unless I have great money or great time I am not going to be as effective alone as I would be with others. And even if I *were* alone the chances are I would immediately try to get a group together to maximize my effectiveness. And that would simply be another church. "Where two or three are gathered in my name, there am I in the midst of them."

My life is abundant when it includes other people. I include *more* people when I join the church. "For God so loved the *world.*" I am reminded that I have to get in there and try to love everybody. You can't get much more abundant than that. The church are the people who keep each other reaching for *that* kind of abundance.

You join the church for the other *in* the church and *beyond* the church. You join the church to do something in your life about other people. And you do that because you know that doing something about other people makes *you* a better person. Why *not* join an organization that makes you better?

It is not a choice between the bad life and the good. That is not the choice at all. It is a choice between the good life and a better one. Jesus is after that better life. "I came that you may have life, and have it abundantly." Insofar as the church mediates Jesus, the church is *essential* to the better life.

The problem, of course, is that the church so often does *not* mediate Jesus. It does *not* offer other people. It does *not* challenge its members to be for themselves by being for others. It does *not* challenge them to live abundantly by living for others.

Frankly, I wouldn't *want* to join an organization that talked about abundant life but did not offer it. I wouldn't want to belong to an organization that did not stimulate and irritate and agitate me to live more abundantly by including other people in my living. The church are the people who will do *anything* to include other people.

The *job* of the church is to make humans human. Abundant life means being what you are—not more than you are. Jesus didn't challenge people to be superhuman. He challenged them to be themselves. His invitations are not impossible. His commands are not idealistic. His sermons are not out of the question. "I came that you may have life, and have it abundantly." All he wanted was for people to *be* who they *were*.

All right. But can't you get all this without the church? And if so many churches are not offering it, wouldn't you get it *better outside* the church? The only answer is to say that if you can get other people better outside the church, then stay out of the church. But you will have to be ruthless with yourself. Is there any other group, you must ask yourself, which challenges you to *"deny* yourself and take up your *cross?"* Is there any other group which challenges you to be for others *that much?*

III

It is at the point of *that much* that I get a *third* thing from the church which I don't get anywhere else. I get the transcendent. I have moved from self-interest to self-denial to self-fulfillment. It may not always happen or even regularly happen, but in the church it can happen. This is the kind of movement that is abundant living. This is the kind of movement that helps me be who I am, or at least begin to be who I am.

I join a church because I am bothered by the question of God.

I join a church to *be* bothered by the question of God. Now this does not mean that if I am out of the church I do not have the question. What it does mean is that if I am in the church I *will* have the question and the question will *not* let me go.

It is the biggest question in life. The question about job, the question about college, the question about family, the question about peace—none of these, big as they are, is as big as the question about God. It is the question about God that makes a man a man. A man is *not* a man until he asks the God-question. To be a man *is* to ask the God-question. It is to live as abundantly as possible and include *God* in my living.

Yes, I can ask the God-question apart from the church. But the point is, *will* I? And it is a crucial point. I can take myself seriously apart from the church. I can take others seriously apart from the church. And I can take God seriously apart from the church. But the question is, *will* I?

Frankly, I am *not* sure that I will. Human nature being what it is, it is far from clear that a person who does not *keep at it* will ask the God-question with anywhere near the profundity of a person who does. More than likely he will either be content with a provisional answer or will give the whole thing up by leaving God to the theologians the way he leaves politics to the politicians.

But is that *enough* if I am going to live as abundantly as I can? I am not at all sure that it is. I am not at all sure that abundant living—really human living—can ever exclude God. Insofar as the church includes God, I need the church.

Again, the trouble is that the church so often *excludes* God, just as it so often excludes other people and wholeness. Indeed it has been called man's last hiding place from God. We do everything in our churches to avoid the transcendent.

Why? Because we fear it. We are afraid of the control it could have over us. It is hard to see how abundant life could be to let go of life. Or it is hard to see—and this is not fear but despair —how there can be a dimension of height as well as a dimension of breadth and depth.

Most of us will do *anything* to avoid the God-question. And it just may be that we need the church to *keep* us asking it. The church *are* the people who ask the God-question. They are also the people who begin to get an answer in the Man and in men. Again, you can get the answer apart from the church. But *does* the answer come to those who do not ask the question? *Does* it come to those who may not even *want* it because they are not willing to take the *risk* of abundant living?

The *job* of the church is to communicate the transcendent. It is to declare *God* in what happens between men. It is to say that what happens between men for beauty, truth, justice, peace *is* God. And it is to get out there and make beauty, truth, justice, peace.

But can't you do all those things without the church? Yes, if I *will*. But I must be extraordinary indeed if I can. Even Jesus needed other people. He formed the first church. He got twelve men. He couldn't do what he did, feel what he felt, think what he thought, be who he was without the church. *His* life couldn't be abundant without the church.

The church are the people who keep me asking the God-question. They are the people who keep me taking risks for other people. They are the people who keep me honest about myself.

13

The Church as Slave

What does the church do that other institutions do not or cannot or will not do?

I

The answer begins with the church's founder. What did Jesus do that other people did not or could not or would not do? Jesus was a slave. He "emptied himself," Paul wrote, "taking the form of a slave" (Phil. 2:7).

Now slavery is not a pretty image. There are many nicer things we could say about Jesus. He was a teacher. He was a leader. He was a man of God. He loved children. All of which would be true, but would they be true enough?

What Jesus did that other people did not do was voluntarily to become a slave. He denied himself. He emptied himself. He poured himself out. He gave everything to become nothing. He even gave his life, and the symbol of emptiness we have kept is of the slave on his cross.

It went back into the reaches of history. An ancient poet had written of his nation that it was a suffering servant. "He poured out his life to death," the poet had written (Isa. 53:12). It said what people felt. Jesus made the poem his. He did what the poem said.

And they would not believe it. It was one thing to write it. It was another thing to do it. No one voluntarily enslaved himself. No one poured himself out until nothing was left. No one denied himself, when the important thing in life was to affirm yourself.

* * *

Jesus affirmed others, not himself. "I am among you as one who serves," he said. He waited on *them* at table. He washed *their* feet. It was an utterly new thing, that a man who could have been a king chose to be a slave.

It was disillusioning. Their illusion was that he would lead them to freedom. In reality he showed them how to be slaves. Their illusion was that he would be himself. In reality he was a man for others. Their illusion was that he would fulfill himself. In reality he "emptied himself." It was an utterly new thing.

* * *

He also affirmed God. He declared his dependence. He did not vaunt his independence. God *was* what he depended upon to be a man for others. When he bowed at their feet it was a symbol of his having already bowed before God. God *was* what he bowed before. God *was* what he submitted to. God *was* what he emptied himself with.

Thus in this man the key *psychological* virtue was self-denial. The key *sociological* virtue was service. And the key *theological* virtue was obedience. All were subsumed in the image of the slave and the symbol of the cross.

II

The church are the people who deny themselves. It is preposterous, of course, but there it is.

. . . *You also* ought to wash one another's feet. For I have given you an example, that you also should do as I have done to you. (John 13:14)

If any man would come after me, let him deny himself and take up his cross. . . . (Matt. 16:24)

Whoever would be first among you must be your *slave*. . . . (Matt. 20:27)

Paul, a *slave* of Jesus Christ. (Rom. 1:1)

James, a *slave* of God and . . . Christ. (James. 1:1)

Peter, a *slave* . . . of Jesus Christ. (2 Pet. 1:1)

Jude, a *slave* of . . . Jesus Christ. (Jude 1:1)

The church is a community based on denying itself. We are not emptied pitchers waiting to be filled. We are filled pitchers waiting to be emptied. The church *are* the people who empty themselves.

It seems to violate all we know in psychology. They called the first church members morons (1 Cor. 1:18, 23). It is moronic to deny yourself. Your business in life is to affirm yourself. If you deny yourself you will get such a bad self-image you won't be able to function.

But is that true? Paul, James, Peter, John, these men who denied themselves—the world has not been the same since. "They turned the world upside down," the Greeks said in a Greek city about these moronic people who were doing it all backward.

How fragile *is* a martyr's ego? How low *was* Jesus' self-image? Did Paul's moronic behavior vitiate his effectiveness? Did Peter's?

The church are the people who deny themselves. Everything they do is measured by their self-denial. As we have seen, their profit is their loss. Their income is their outgo. It's moronic. For a man to give away 10 percent of his income—he's out of his mind. For a man to put his body on the line and empty himself for someone else, he's got to be crazy, psychologically destroyed rather than made.

The opposite of the moron was the "sophisticate." It is not sophisticated to empty yourself. It is not sophisticated to be a slave. It is not sophisticated to put yourself aside for somebody else.

But the sophisticates lost. Their religion is gone. It didn't make it out of the third century. The temples are gone; the church remains. The oracle who said "Know thyself" is forgotten. The man who said "Love your neighbor" lives.

The issue cannot be compromised. "If any man would come after me," the man said, "let him deny himself." He did not say, "Let him affirm himself." He did not say, "Let him be himself and *then* he will become a man for others." He said, "Let him be a man for others and *then* he will be himself."

Whoever would be first among you must be your *slave*.
You also ought to wash one another's feet.

*   *   *

The church are the people who affirm other people. It is preposterous, but there it is. "Whoever would be first among you must be your slave." It is the image of the slave that puts the institution in the right perspective.

The church is an institution that exists for the benefit of those who are *not* its members. It is an institution that lives by dying. It is an institution that "pours out its life to death." It is an institution organized for the other rather than for the self.

The political party, the corporation, the lobby—they are self-interest groups. They are organized to promote their self-interest. The church is organized for the other, not itself. The trouble with the church always comes when the church becomes another self-interest group. It may *begin* that way, with members joining because it is in their own interest. But it does not *end* that way. Their own interest, they find, is to be interested in *others*.

One reason 75 percent of America is saying that religion is losing its influence on American life is that the church has become sophisticated. It has become what it is not. It has organized for itself rather than for others. It has spent more on itself than it has on others. It has studied when it should have shared. It has shared when it should have served.

What it has *not* done is to present to the world the image of the suffering servant. What it has *not* done is to be willing to die. What it has *not* done is to follow the example of its founder when he specifically told it—us—to follow his example.

You join the fellowship for the *other* in the fellowship. You join it for the other *beyond* the fellowship. "You also ought to wash one another's feet." You also ought to deny yourself. You also ought to take up your cross, the symbol par excellence of self-emptying.

Your service is to feed the hungry. Your service is to clothe the naked. Your service is to care for the sick and the imprisoned and the stranger. That is what I am calling your service. "I am among you as one who serves." And you are among your neighbors as "one who serves."

The church are the people who serve. "I came not to be served but to serve." "I have given you an example." The church are the people who put the other before the self. There is no compromise. "If any man would come after me, let him deny himself." We will or we will not do it. It is an either-or. Either we will be slaves or we will not. Either we will live for the other or we will not.

*

It is not easy. But no one said it would be easy. If it were easy it would not be attractive. It would not compel. It would not inspire. The church are the people who encourage each other in doing what seems impossible to do.

This is the big argument—that Jesus aimed at a mark which was not there in human nature. It was Robert Frost's criticism of President Wilson and the League of Nations. It was one thing for Jesus. It is another thing for us.

But the argument does not hold, and it does not hold precisely because the attraction has held. Something draws us, and has drawn us for centuries, to be *more* for others than we are for ourselves. Something responds to the image of the slave or it would not have survived as the most compelling image in the history of the world. Something responds to the symbol of the cross as the highest form of human conduct.

How much of myself *do* I empty? The church are the people who ask that question and then report to each other the answers they have found that week. The extraordinary thing is that the more a person gives the more he receives. He only has what he gives. But the receiving is *after* the giving, not before.

You join a church for what you can give, not for what you can receive. But you don't always *know* that until you have joined, as we saw in the preceding chapter, for what you can get. Basically, you never join a church for peace of mind. You join it to serve others, and you may or may not get peace of mind.

Receiving is a *by-product* of giving. Psychology is a *by-product* of sociology. "Be yourself" is *not* a Christian sentiment. "Be a man for others" is. When I am for others, *then* I am for self. When I find others, *then* I find self. "If any man would come after me, let him *deny* himself." But you don't *know* that until you have tried it the other way around. The church are the people who try it the other way around and then are surprised by each other. They are the people who begin selfishly and end altruistically. They went in for what they could get; they came out with what they can give. *Jesus* has happened.

We find the Christ in the other, not in the self. Christianity is not a religion where you find Jesus only "inside." It is where you find him also outside. The Judeo-Christian is primarily a sociological religion. It is not primarily a psychological religion. The "power of positive thinking" is only secondarily Christian. Christianity is the power of positive acting, from which you may or may not get positive thinking.

When I am a slave, then I am free. When I find the other, then I find myself. "You were called to *freedom,* brethren." And then, in the same sentence: "Through love be *slaves* of one another" (Gal. 5:13).

*

The church are the people who are *way* out in front in explor-ing how to be for others. The church does *anything* that will enable it to *be* more effectively for others. It is no accident that the greatest image we have in mid-twentieth-century America of service to others was given us by a churchman who then went on to his cross.

He had immense gifts. He gave them away. "As each has received a gift," Peter wrote, "employ it for one another." The Greek word for gift was "charisma." Martin Luther King was charismatic not because he was a great leader, but because he was a great giver. A Christian is *expected* to be charismatic. Churches *are* charismatic or they are not churches.

What have we done in this country, that we hoard our gifts, that we put the private over the public, the national ahead of the international—our national "self-interest," as we call it, ahead of half the world that goes to bed hungry? "Nowhere in the world," de Tocqueville wrote of us, "were there so many ambitious people with such low ambitions." Why?

Because we have been Greek when we should have been He-brew, we have been Western when we should have been Eastern, we have been non-Christian when we should have been Christian, we have put the self ahead of the other, the individual ahead of the group, the prince ahead of the slave, the right of one man to belch his pollution before the right of other men not to breathe it.

"How can a man be happy when he has to serve someone?" It was a Greek question, asked by the sophists, the sophisticates. It was asked so often it became a formula.

The church are the people who deny themselves and affirm others.

* * *

They are also the people who affirm God. God *is* what we depend on to be men for others. God *is* what enslaves us.

God *is* what we empty ourselves with.

The Greek gods are gone, the gods who made no demands, who did not dare to enslave, who expected no obedience. The Hebrew God remains; indeed, it is now the God of Greece as well as of Israel. The God who expects, the God who commands, the God who enslaves remains.

The word "church" comes from the Greek word for "lord." The Greek word for lord meant "the superiority to which there must be submission."[1] God *is* superior to men. God *is* beyond man's ability to grasp and therefore must be bowed before.

To this day we bow our heads when we think of God. It is a symbol of obedience. It is a symbol of slavery. The slave bowed before his master. God *is* what we do not have power over. The Greeks rose and overpowered their gods. The Hebrews fell and were enslaved. There was no kneeling in the Greek religion. There was no Suffering Servant. There was no obedience. There was only freedom, the freedom of every man to be himself; *not* the obedience of every man to be for others.

To this day the Greek and the Hebrew struggle in us. When will the Hebrew win? When will we become slaves? God *is* what enables a man to live for others. The church *are* the people who live for others.

14

The Church As Servant

There are those who are saying it is all over for the church.
They point to the decline in attendance. They point to the
weakness in giving. They point to a membership that cannot
keep pace with the population.

They also point to the seminaries. Enrollment is at an all-time
high, but church work at an all-time low. Of recent graduates
of Union Seminary in New York, 80 percent have rejected the
parish ministry as a profession. The reason they give, according
to Union's president, is that they are committed to social
change.[1]

The biggest social fiction I have discovered [writes a college student]
is the Christian church. There are so many fallacies, and so much that
is farcical about today's church, that it seems worthless to attend one.
The "Is God Dead?" group fights with the "God is Love" group, and
the result is a watered-down, apathetic, really pathetic group of social
institutions that dare to call themselves Christian churches.

*

What's the matter? *One* reason for the trouble is that people
are joining churches not on confession but on confusion of faith.
They do not know what is expected of them when they join, and
the results are the usual three-ring churches—one-third committed, one-third peripheral, and one-third out.

Another reason is that people are not getting a message in
churches but a massage. It has long been evident to the percep-
tive that churches which feed peace-of-mind pabulum every
week are soft churches.

A *third* reason is that once people do join they are put in the wrong jobs. The present flaccidity of the church is ironic testimony to the pyrrhic victory of a fat bureaucracy.

A *fourth* reason it may be all over for the church is that the church is behind the times. It has failed to keep up. It is an anachronism. "The church," said an executive vice president, "is the most conservative institution in America." And he did not mean it as a compliment.

People are leaving the church right and left. Literally. The conservatives leave because the church is doing too much. The liberals leave because the church is doing too little.

There is a *fifth* reason it may be all over for the church, and maybe this one goes to the heart of the problem. The church no longer commands the moral respect of the world. Particularly it does not command the moral respect of the young and the black. Why? Because the church so often stands for what is popular over what is right. It stands for what is comfortable over what must be done. It stands for the status quo over revolution.

Now to be sure, there is much in the status that should remain. There is much that is right in the fabric of most American communities. What the young and the black and the dispossessed are saying to the church is: Go out and fight for the rest of the right. Do not be content with what has been achieved. "Press on," said St. Paul.

The trouble is that the fight has been drained from so many churches. You rarely hear of churches taking stands on social issues. You rarely read of churches in jails and ghettos binding up the wounds of the community. You rarely see church members doing the kinds of things that need to be done to command the moral respect of the world. As a black woman, who was also young, said to a visiting church member in a jail: "Church members are all mouth. Christians are all heart."

II

The church must become a servant. That is how it will recapture the moral respect of the world. It is the servant spirit that is lacking in today's church. It is the loss of the servant virtues, among other things, that has engendered the loss of respect for the church.

Unlike its founder, the church has not been willing to die. Unlike its founder, the church has not been willing to develop the virtues that command the respect of the world. At least not now. The first-century church was a different matter. That church went out, as it says in the Book of Acts, and "turned the world upside down."

What are the servant virtues?

*

One is *obedience*. "We take every thought captive," Paul said, "to obey Christ" (2 Cor. 10:5). As we have seen, he called himself the "slave of Christ." The grestest virtue of the slave is obedience.

He got it from Christ himself. Christ was the Suffering Servant. He was the one person who was so enslaved to God that he obeyed God in everything. Christ was the obedient man. "Not my will," he prayed, "but thine be done."

Christ obeyed God. Christians obey Christ. He is an example of what it means to obey. Therefore Christians go where Christ went. They do what he did. They fight what he fought.

"Go," Christ said. It was not a suggestion, it was a command, and we will or will not obey. "Love," he said. It was not a suggestion. He specifically called it a commandment. And we will or will not obey.

The servant church is an obedient church. "Do you promise to follow where you see him lead?" people are asked when they join churches. If they say Yes, which they always do, then they *will* follow, and they *will* go wherever he leads, at great risk to themselves.

The words that tell of the ministry of Christ [writes Episcopal lawyer William Stringfellow] are words of sorrow, poverty, rejection, radical unpopularity. They are words of agony. It seems ridiculous to apply such words to the ministry of churches nowadays.[2]

The servant church is an obedient church. In the obedience is the élan. In the obedience is the esprit. The esprit de corps. To be a marine is to be proud. To be a graduate of a service (sic) academy is to be proud.

The day had been one of confusion [wrote General Eisenhower of his first day at West Point] . . . but when we raised our right hands and repeated the official oath, there was no confusion. A feeling came over me that the expression "The United States of America" would now and henceforth mean something different. From here on, it would be the nation I would be serving, not myself. . . . Across half a century, I can look back and see a raw-boned, gawky Kansas boy from the farm country earnestly repeating the words that would make him a cadet.[3]

"As you have always obeyed," Paul wrote. "If you love me," Christ said, "you will keep my *commandments.*" "You are my friends, *if* you do what I command you." Writes a commentator:

Before men can be changed they must obey. Obedience is the one form of self-surrender that hurts enough to prove that self has really given up some of its own will. It may be forced, and lack the true spirit, but it is the first step in putting a man where the word of God can be done through him.[4]

Dietrich Bonhoeffer left the safety of that same Union Seminary in New York and returned to his native Germany to fight the Nazis. He was obedient to what Christ had called him to do. He knew that the risk was death, just as the serviceman knows that the risk is death.

*

Another servant virtue is *discipline*. A church that means business is a disciplined church. It is clean and lithe and ready to meet the needs of the time. It is a taut and disciplined cadre whose self-discipline commands the respect of the world.

To be a disciple is to be disciplined. The words come from the same root. At the heart of every great moral achievement is self-discipline. It was discipline that kept Washington and the others at Valley Forge. It was discipline that kept the early church in the arena.

Where is the discipline in the modern church? It is in the corporation. Why is it not in the church? It is in the political party. Why is it not in the church? It is in the military. Why is it not in the church?

One reason is that the church makes no demands on its members. A man could never join a corporation and do nothing. He would be fired. He could never run for office and do nothing. He would lose the next election. He could never be an officer and do nothing. He would not be promoted.

Certain things are demanded of people who join the organization of the Suffering Servant. If they are not suffering servants too—in the giving of everything from time to money to self—then they have no business belonging to that man's organization.

Christ made demands upon people. "If any man would come after me, let him deny himself." It is the penultimate demand. No one denies himself fully, but if we are not at least beginning the process, what right have we to call ourselves Christians?

Another reason that discipline is gone from the modern church is that the church, when it does make demands, makes weak ones. New member classes are swooped on by flower committees, greeter committees, usher committees. But where is the challenge to go to the jail? Where is the challenge to join the political party? To solder the Christian ethic onto your job?

To have $200,000 benevolence fund drives to equal—or better, exceed—what we have already spent on ourselves in our building fund drives?

Without such challenges, insitutions begin to dominate people, means dominate ends, form dominates spirit. Now we are going to have to deinstitutionalize, in many cases, in order to rehumanize.

James Reston, one of our most lucid critics, puts it this way:

The main problem is that the leaders of America—not only in government but in the universities, the churches, the big corporations, the newspapers, and the television networks—are so overwhelmed by the problem of doing things that they have little time left to think about what they are doing. Operations dominate purposes.[5]

What is the purpose of the church? To be a suffering servant. "Through love," Paul wrote, "be servants of one another." "Whoever would be first among you," Christ said, "must be your slave."

What is the operation of the church to accomplish this purpose? Surely one operation is self-discipline, because without self-discipline we just do not have what it takes to be slaves. The imperious claims of the self are such, human nature being what it is, that without constant self-discipline the self will become a god, not a slave, and the Faustian-Promethean-Adamitic tragedy will be enacted all over again.

Christ's discipline was immense. He never wavered from his purpose, that of being a suffering servant. He never turned aside. He never became loose, flaccid, weak. Christ was tough. And without that same toughness we are never going to do what he did; the servant church will never be a fact but a dream; and we will never be able to command the moral respect of the world.

*

A third servant virtue is *sacrifice*. It is the summons to die, if need be, in the service of that which is greater than the self. "If any man would come after me, let him deny himself and take up his *cross.*" It is the ultimate demand.

The cross is the symbol of the Christian church. It is a symbol of sacrifice. It is a symbol of suffering service. It is a symbol of how, when we pay the ultimate price, there can be new life.

The trouble is that the cross, in church after church, has been prettied. It is no longer two man-killing hunks of wood. It is either gold or shellacked or orbed or something else it should not be. The moral demand for sacrifice has been buried under the aesthetic demand for beauty.

And that, of course, is a very serious thing. The good, in the Judeo-Christian tradition, if it comes down to that, must always beat the beautiful. The trouble is that the beautiful, as often happens in the church and elsewhere, has been beating the good.

The cross is not a symbol of beauty but of sacrifice. In the ugliness of the cross, of the man-killing sacrifice, is the most beautiful thing that has ever been done.

The question then comes to the servant church: How much are *you* willing to sacrifice? How much are *you* willing to say that suffering love is the highest value in the world? How much are *you* willing to pay up personally? How much are *you* willing to put *your* body on the line?

The answer is by no means clear. It could go either way. There is evidence on both sides. For the pessimist, as the late H. Richard Niebuhr put it, the trouble with American religion is that "a God without wrath brought men without sin into a kingdom without judgment through . . . a Christ without a cross."[6]

For the optimists, as another scholar has written, there is the original call to the church, which, remarkably, still has its fire.

The Son calls for *unreserved* decision for God and gathers around Him a band of "stormtroopers" (Matt. 11.12) who leave *everything,* and follow Him and love God with *passionate* devotion. He creates a *new* people of God which renounces *all* hatred and force and, with an unconquerable resolve to *love*, treads the way of *sacrifice* in face of *all* opposition. And He Himself dies, as the ancient tradition tells us, with a request for ths hostile world (Luke 23.34).[7]

The challenge to the church is to take up its cross and be willing to die that its moral position may live. Institutions have been known to sacrifice. It is through symbols of sacrifice—like paring church building programs, having benevolence fund drives for those who need the money more—that the church can recapture the moral respect of the world. It is through sacrifice that the church can create something more beautiful than we ever dared to believe.

"If any man would come after me, let him deny himself and take up his cross."

A man from a church went into the ghetto on his lunch hour to tutor in a slum school. He was assigned the class toughie in the first grade. On his second visit, as the man and the boy bent over the flashcards in the hallway of that elementary school, the little boy reached up and put his arms around the neck of the man and kissed him.

That's the church.

15

The Church as Sleeping Giant

The church is in trouble. Membership lags. Giving is weak. Attendance is down. Clergy quit. Laymen leave. Seminarians refuse ordination.

Young people laugh at the church as irrelevant. Black people write the church off as a liar. Hungry people view the church as uncaring.

Politicians scoff at the church as "incompetent." Businessmen spurn it as "unrealistic." Military men scorn it as "idealistic."

The church is peripheral when it should be central. It is on the edge when it should be at the heart. It is silent when it should speak. It dallies when it should act. "Simon," Jesus asked Peter in the garden, "are you asleep? Could you not watch one hour?" (Mark 14:37)

*

The church is a sleeping giant. It has the equipment; it lacks the drive. It has the power; it lacks the will. It has the mind; it lacks the heart.

The challenge to the church is to be converted. It is to convert resources into energy, indolence into action, sleeping into waking, death into life.

The stunning thing is that it can. The church is a sleeping giant, but it can wake. The church is a sleeping giant, but it is a giant. The disciples awoke. And the world has not been the same since.

I

Consider *first* the church's intellectual equipment. It is staggering. People sit in churches with all sorts of advanced degrees. Chemists, physicists, biologists. Attorneys, doctors, dentists. Engineers, executives, architects.

Even where there are no advanced degrees the brainwork is impressive. A mother, for instance, is one of the world's most important people. By the age of four, we are told, a child has formed half the intelligence he will have at maturity.[1] By the age of four a child's IQ becomes so stable it is a fairly accurate indicator of his IQ at 17.[2] "Behind every highly able person," it has been concluded, "there stands someone who stimulated him during his preschool years."[3]

Scratch a school board anywhere in the country and you are likely to find church members on it. As we have seen, the *majority* will probably be church members. It is the same with our leadership in colleges, businesses, corporations, governments.

Are we going to sleep with our brain power, or wake?

*

Why couldn't the local church be another think tank? Two billion dollars a year go into America's think tanks. We can get the thinkers for nothing because they are in the churches. All they have to do is think.

Let's play games. Let's do our R and D (research and development). Let's list objectives, then list resources, then determine how best to use the resources to gain the objectives. That's all systems analysis is, and 50 percent of the men in a given church will be using it every day.

What about Kepener and Tregoe? What about Drucker? What about reversing, which means changing the problem? "If you can't find a solvent for ink," said the founder of GE's research lab, "change the ink." What about lateral thinking? If you can't go through a problem, go around it. According to a recent article in IBM's *Think:*

An old grandmother, knitting by the fire, was being persecuted by the toddler of the family, who insisted on tangling up her wool. The child was put into a playpen but howled so much that he had to be taken out again. So the grandmother decided to sit in the playpen herself, leaving the child outside.[4]

*

The question, of course, is whether the church ever *can* become a think tank. On the one hand, the church was responsible for the first universities. On the other hand, it was responsible for the Inquisition. The church is notorious for preserving the old rather than thinking hard for the new. So often it does not risk. It does not dare. It does not adventure.

Where are the Cape Kennedys of the church? Where are the RANDs? Where are the Hudson Institutes? How many men think as hard in religion as they do in business? How many women are as creative at church as they are at home?

Can it be done? The answer is moot. So often in the church we don't learn any more, we merely consolidate our prejudices. So often in religion we feel we have to have the last word rather than the latest. Science knows only the latest word, not the last. "My people are destroyed," wrote Hosea, "for lack of knowledge" (Hos. 4:6).

*

Can the church become a think tank? Yes. Lest we assume it debilitating to think hard beyond our jobs: it has been discovered in a study of 424 executives whose average age was 52 that "the brain simply does not get exhausted from overwork."[5]

Any decline of mental powers with age . . . is more likely to result from the brain's getting too little rather than too much work.[6]

"How can I know?" was Montaigne's motto. "I am still learning," was Michelangelo's motto. "No man really becomes a fool," said Charles Steinmetz, "until he stops asking questions."

What is the meaning of my life? What is its transcendent principle? How can the church communicate the transcendent? "He who would succeed," said Aristotle, "must ask the right preliminary questions." "Simon," asked Jesus, "are you asleep?"

II

Consider *second* the church's emotional equipment. It is extraordinary. More to the point, it is unique.

We should never forget that Christianity made its way in the Greek and Roman world not only through its message and ideas, but also through the demonstration of its fellowship, an utterly new thing; and that many were attracted to the fellowship before they understood the message or fully accepted it.[7]

The church has love, Christian love, *agape, koinonia,* fellowship. Other institutions may exist for fellowship. What the church has that other institutions may lack is, as we have seen, concern for the other in the fellowship rather than the self. One is in it *for* the other in the fellowship.

It is our care for the helpless [wrote Tertullian in the second century] our practice of lovingkindness, that brands us in the eyes of many of our opponents. "Only look," they say, "look how they love one another. . . . Look how they are prepared to die for one another."[8]

*

Can the church release the love that it has? On the one hand the answer is moot. Many would argue that our track record is poor. They have their evidence—from burnings to witch hunts to fat American churches—and it is hard to contest.

On the other hand the answer is Yes. In spite of its past, even in spite of its present, the church can surely become what it was meant to be. John Gardner's rule No. 8 for organizational renewal is that the organization be interested in what it is going to become and not in what it has been.[9]

First there is what Bonhoeffer called "the ministry of listening."[10]

The first service that one owes to others in the fellowship consists in listening to them. Just as love to God begins with listening to His Word, so the beginning of love for the brethren is learning to listen to them.[11]

Next there is what he called "the ministry of helpfulness."[12]

We must be ready to allow ourselves to be interrupted by God. God will be constantly crossing our paths with claims and petitions. We may pass them by . . . reading the Bible. [But] when we do that we pass by the visible sign of the Cross raised athwart our path to show that, not our way, but God's way must be done.[13]

Then there is what he called "the ministry of bearing."[14]

It is the fellowship of the Cross to experience the burden of the other. If one does not experience it, the fellowship he belongs to is not Christian.[15]

III

Consider *third* the church's action equipment. It, too, is extraordinary. Not only is the church concerned for those in the fellowship, it is also concerned for those *beyond* the fellowship. Indeed, Archbishop Temple went so far as to say: "The church is the only organization in the world which exists for the benefit of those who are *not* its members."

The church's power is enormous. Almost a billion people, nearly a third of the world, belong to the church. In America alone 320,000 meetings are held every Sunday. As we have seen, they are held in facilities (land and buildings) worth $80 billion.[16] Over $7 billion a year is contributed, nearly half of all

U.S. charitable giving.[17] Ninety-nine percent of America's corporations, according to the *Harvard Business Review,* earn a pretax profit of less than $500,000 a year.[18]

To repeat: No other group in America is in such close contact with so much of America. No other group is in such close contact with the power structure. In community after community and state after state the church *is* the power structure. That is, the people in power belong to the church, just as the people in think tanks and the people in families belong to the church.

But there is more. Not only is the church a catalyst for a man's most important thinking, about the meaning of his life. Not only is it a catalyst for a man's most important feeling, the emotion of love. It is also a catalyst for a man's channeling that thinking and feeling into some of the most significant acting he has ever done. The question is, will he do it? "Simon, are you asleep?"

*

Again, the answer is moot. Many say that the church will continue to sleep. It will not use its brain. It will not use its heart. And it will not use its muscle. The church, say the young, is not worth confronting any more. We will go after the university instead.

The churches provide an easy rationale for well-meaning white people [reads the 1967 report of a major city's Commission on Human Development] who do not have the courage or understanding to involve themselves with the Negro people in our city. As a whole, the church has not accepted a responsibility in human relations. It *could* have real power in this field. To the contrary, the churches have contributed greatly to the gap between the white and Negro communities.[19]

Naturally there are many who do not agree with the report. But whether they agree or not is secondary. What is primary is that writers of such reports and countless others do agree. It is the old objection back in the Book of Timothy about "holding the form of religion but denying the power of it" (2 Tim. 3:5).

*

Obviously it is time to get the power back, to wake the giant up, to get the action out there and visible. There are many ways this can be done and is being done. One way is less a strategy, perhaps, than an attitude.

There is far more to a church's power than its obvious clout —economic, demographic, political—in a community. The church's strength is its weakness. Its power is its frailty. Its life is its death. "He who would lose his life will find it."

While the disciples slept, Jesus prayed. "Father . . . not what I will, but what thou wilt." Jesus was willing to be killed. He was willing to suffer. The Greek words describing him as he went into the garden depict the utmost in horror and suffering.

It is not easy for a church to give when, like any institution, it wants to receive. It is not easy for the church to spend itself when, like any institution, it wants to amass for itself. So the church suffers as it tries to give and as it allows itself to be spent. *One,* it spends more on others than it does on itself. *Two,* it forms itself into a Third Force. *Three,* it moves on the action priorities in its community.

It is precisely this suffering, as the church gives itself in love to the uttermost, that the world understands. The world feels. The world is moved to respond. The church, like its founder, is a suffering servant.

Impossible? So was the flight to the moon. "Rise," Jesus said, "let us be going." Giant, awake!

16

What's Right with the Church

In a day when it is fashionable to criticize the church, occasionally it is refreshing to praise it. To be sure, there is much that is wrong with the church. But there is also much that is right. And it is high time the Cassandras were met on their own ground.

I

One, the church is the biggest organization in the world. As we saw, it has nearly a billion members, almost a third of the world. It is the only organization in the world that is in every country in the world. And it is the only organization in the world that turns out its members for a world-wide meeting every week.

It is the only organization in America that is in nearly every city, town, village, and hamlet. There are more churches than post offices. There is no other organization in the country which comes anywhere near the church in size, with its 130 million members, or 63 percent of the population.

Christianity's only world-wide rival in size is Communism. Like Christianity, Communism embraces a third of the world. But four-fifths of these people are in only two countries, China and Russia; of all these people only 5 percent actually belong to the Communist party; and Communism has, of course, been around for only 50 years.

The Christian church is mammoth.

It is also durable. *It* has been around for 2,000 years, and it is likely to be around for another 2,000. Hinduism, Buddhism, Judaism are all older than Christianity, but none so combines length and breadth. There are three times more Christians than Hindus, six times more Christians than Buddhists, eighty times more Christians than Jews.

Christianity's nearest competitor in size is Islam, but again, there are more than twice as many Christians as Mohammedans, Islam is not nearly so widespread as Christianity, and it is six hundred years younger.

Now to be sure, Christianity is losing ground. Where 35 percent of the world was Christian in 1900, only 20 percent according to a demographer, will be in 2000.[1] Islam is growing fast. Nevertheless, the fact of the matter is that the Christian church is still the single biggest organization in the world.

II

Two, it is also the smallest. Paradoxically, no matter how big the church becomes, it remains small. No matter how huge, it remains intimate.

"Where two or three are gathered in my name," its founder said. "If *one* member suffers," its first great missionary wrote, "all suffer together; if *one* member is honored, all rejoice together." The Christian church can have a billion people in it, but when just one of its members is in trouble the others are there. They hurt, too.

That is the genius of the church. There are plenty of large organizations in the world. But how many of them have that kind of concern for the smallest member, be he a year old or ninety, black or white, rich or poor, American or Ethiopian?

"Bear one another's burdens," the missionary wrote. And that is what the church does. More to the point, it is what the church do. They demonstrate by their fellowship that they care about people. "They devoted themselves to the . . . fellowship," we read about the first church. And it was that kind of intimate caring that enabled them to go out and "turn the world upside down."

Now, to be sure, we all know people who have gone out of churches grumbling that "nobody spoke to me." Translated, this always means, of course: "I didn't speak to anybody." And we all know instances when the church has erred in its fellowship. A man confessed his homosexuality to a small group of Christians, they were shocked, they couldn't handle it lovingly, and he committed suicide.

Nevertheless, the church, mammoth in extent, is singular in intent. Its concern is every one of its members. Its concern is to be an organism rather than an organization, which is precisely the kind of biological metaphor Jesus and Paul chose for it. They never spoke of the church in institution-ese. It was the *body* of Christ, the *koinonia,* the *fellowship,* that went out there and turned the world upside down—and still can.

III

Three, the church is the most revolutionary organization in the world. No other organization is so dedicated to *changing* people's lives. As a matter of fact, a *condition* of joining is that you are changed or that you are being changed. The Christian church does not want us as we are. That, frankly, is not good enough. It wants us as Christ wants us—reconciled to God, to others, and to ourselves. "God was in Christ," Paul, the missionary, wrote, "reconciling the world to himself" (2 Cor. 5:19).

Most organizations want you as you are. They don't want to change you. If you're a Democrat they certainly don't want you changing to Republican. If you're an American the country doesn't want you changing to Russian. If you're a Yankee fan the Yankees don't want you changing to a Red Sox fan.

The Christian church wants us to change. It is that revolutionary. Its *job* as an organization is to get us to change. "Repent," said its founder in his first sermon, and Peter in his. The word meant, literally, "change."

Change to what? Change to reconciliation—where Jews and Gentiles were sitting down in the same house, Roman citizens and slaves, men and women, all sharing for the first time in the fellowship. It was astounding. More than that, as Dr. Luccock wrote, it was "an utterly *new* thing." When Christ gets hold of a man he is a *new* man. "If any one is in Christ, he is a *new* creation; the old has passed away, behold, the *new* has come" (2 Cor. 5:17).

Now, to be sure, there are people in churches who are not changed. There are plenty who are not caught up in the revolution, who have not experienced the new life. Nevertheless, the Christian church is the only organization in the world totally dedicated to changing the total man. Other organizations, as governments and clubs, can change habits, but it is the church that changes lives.

IV

Four, the church is certainly the most presumptuous organization in the world. Not only does it seek to change men. It seeks to change society. The energy of its revolution is such that it cannot stop at changing a man, it has to go on to change the world.

Most of us are interested in biting off about what we can chew. Not so the church. The little church we know at the corner of State and Main is not in business for itself, not even for its own community. It is part of a major conspiracy to take over the world.

So are the Communists, we might say. Or, for that matter, so are the democrats. But there is a difference between a political and a religious conspiracy. The meaning of the one stops with the state, the meaning of the other with God. The one, in other words, depending on your frame of reference, stops short, while the other goes all the way. The one offers a proximate meaning, the other an ultimate.

Now, to be sure, Christians have been notoriously coercive in their conspiracy. The Inquisition and the Crusades are hardly edifying examples of Christian presumption. Nor, for that matter, is colonialism, which often wedded the church to reactionary government. Witness Rhodesia, Angola, America vs. American Indian.

Nevertheless, it is the presumptuous energy of the Christian church that many people are saying is the hope of the world. Why? Because that energy, at its best, consists of a passion for telling about the new life, and what is more important, a passion for living it. When we live the new life, we love; and love, many people are saying, is the hope of the world.

Naive? Perhaps. But surely reconciliation is better than war. Surely love is better than hate. Surely the presumption of the new life is better than the complacency of the old.

The church is that group of people who go out in love to bind up the wounds of the world. It is the church that was there after the Arab-Israeli war, in the desert with the refugees, who were not, note, members of its organization. It is the church that was there after the cyclone in Pakistan. It is the church that was there in Montgomery in 1955 with a bus boycott to try to bring healing to a community that had been torn apart for 150 years.

Why does the church do it? Because it has already been done for them. "We love, because he first loved us"(1 John 4:19). The church does it because God did it. Which means that the church does it because a man, they feel, went the route for them. He gave himself in love to the uttermost. Therefore they are motivated to do the same. And that, the church says, is how it will win the world.

V

Five, the church is the world's most vociferous organization. It is strident about Jesus Christ. It cannot stop talking about him.

It goes everywhere to tell about that man.

The church is not only a community of suffering servants, it is the world's largest speakers' bureau. The word "apostle" meant "one who is sent." The word "missionary" meant "one who is sent." The word "martyr" meant "witness." Wherever the first Christians went they spoke about Christ. They had to speak. They could not keep silent. And that is what got them in trouble. It is also what "turned the world upside down."

"Woe to me," Paul said, "if I do not preach the gospel!" (1 Cor. 9:16.) "Christ has a right to be announced," says a strident Cardinal Wyzinski of Communist Poland, "and we have the right to announce him. No one can shut our mouths."

In the United States alone, 55 million people listen to more than a billion words in sermons every Sunday.[2] Some would argue, of course, that this is a mixed blessing. "Proof of the divinity of the gospel," Woodrow Wilson once observed, "is all the preaching it has survived."

> The Spirit of the Lord is upon me [Jesus quoted],
> because he has anointed me to *preach* good news to the poor.
> (Luke 4:18)

To be sure, the church has often been silent when it should have been vociferous. It was silent in Montgomery for 150 years. It was silent in Selma. It was far too silent in Detroit— Newark—Watts.

Nevertheless it is to the church that men turn, time after time, to speak for them. As Einstein said in reflecting on Hitler:

> Being a lover of freedom I looked to the universities to defend it . . . but no, the universities were immediately silenced. Then I looked to the great editors of the newspapers, but they, like the universities, were silenced in a few short weeks. Then I looked to the individual writers, but they too were mute. Only the Church stood squarely across the path of Hitler's campaign for suppressing the truth. . . . The Church alone had the courage and persistence to stand for intellectual truth and moral freedom. I am forced to confess that what I once despised I now praise unreservedly.[3]

VI

Six, to end where we began, and to give the Cassandras their due, the church is the world's most self-critical organization. No other world organization is founded on the belief in the badness of its members. "All have sinned," Paul wrote, "and fall short of the glory of God" (Rom. 3:23).

This means that every one of the church's programs is suspect. They are all infected with self-interest. Therefore the church is at all times ready to move to new programs.

That, say the Cassandras, is precisely the point. The church is *not* ready. It is notoriously slow in moving to adopt new programs. You may *think* it is so self-critical that it can be flexible, but what about the Pope and the pill? What about the American church and the racial crisis?

The Cassandras are half-right. The other half is that all over the world church program is being retooled. "Let the world write the agenda" is now a cliché in churches. The church is becoming increasingly vulnerable to the world.

Proof is the world-wide outcry *against* the Pope's encyclical. Proof is the millions of dollars churches are pouring into the city. They are establishing everything from black business to black housing and they are moving fast. Never fast enough, to be sure, but fast.

All over the country, through Project Equality, churches are using their tremendous economic clout to patronize only those firms that do not discriminate. They are also demanding—not asking or even requesting, but demanding—that their members go into their urban and suburban ghettos and organize their respective constituencies for meaningful social change. The church *is* becoming the Third Force.

*

Self-criticism means not only that the church's programs are suspect, but that the church itself is ready to die. And that is a most unusual thing to say about an organization. Most organizations are in business to grow, and hopefully to survive forever. Even the American Guppy Association hopes to increase its membership.

So does the church. But there is a difference. Whenever an institutional form gets in the way of its mission, the church is willing to die that the gospel may live. The cross is the church's symbol.

Again, say the Cassandras, that's great in theory but woeful in practice. The church takes just as dim a view of criticism as the rest of man's institutions. It is no more willing to die than the PTA. There are countless churches—and church programs —which have hung on for fifty years when they should have been scratched.

Half-right again. The other half is that Jesus, the disciples, and thousands of the first churchmen were ready to die that the gospel might live. "What you sow," Paul wrote a church on the rocks, "does not come to life unless it dies" (1 Cor. 15:36). "The blood of the martyrs," said that same Tertullian, "is the seed of the church."

The willingness of the church to die is seen in the countless churches that have begun to whittle their memberships. Gone are the days—or at least going—when the church felt it had to have a big membership to be in business as a church. The old standards will no longer do. People in churches who will not revolt and will not presume are increasingly being fired.

That is what "church renewal" is all about. All over the country churches are quietly closing their doors. Not only are a number of churches folding outright. Others are closing their doors on the uncommitted members. If a person has joined a church and has not gotten the message about serving the world, then he is being asked by more and more churches to get the message or get out.

*

Mammoth and intimate, revolutionary and presumptuous, vociferous and self-critical, the church is the world's most powerful organization. It is engaged, as its first members were, in turning the world upside down. May it never be content with less.

17

The Church in 2000

The church was rich. The church was stolid. The church was indifferent. The writer of Revelation was angry.

You are neither cold nor hot [he wrote for the Risen Christ]. . . . So, because you are lukewarm . . . I will spew you out of my mouth. (Rev. 3:15-16)

It was not a pretty picture. But, then, it was not a pretty church.

Laodicea was the financial capital of Asia Minor: its banks were the biggest and best. It was the commercial capital: its clothing industry was world-famous. It was the medical capital: it had perfected a legendary poultice for the eyes.

You say, I am rich, I have prospered, and I need nothing. . . . (Rev. 3:17)

The church in Laodicea was not a church at all. It was a chamber of commerce.

However, the church in Laodicea did make it out of the first century. So did many of the other churches. Some surprising things happened. The same things are going to have to happen now if the church is going to make it into the twenty-first century with anything like the power it had in the first.

I

One, the church lost weight. Its members began to leave. They could not take what the church was telling them they must take if they were to remain church members. It was the time of the persecutions by the emperor Domitian. And the church was saying through men like the writer of Revelation that there can be no compromise. Either you affirm that Jesus is Lord or that the emperor is. If Jesus is Lord you stay in the church and risk your death. If the emperor is Lord you leave the church and save your life.

America is rich. Its banks are the biggest and best. Its industry is world-famous. Its medical discoveries are legendary. And its churches are indifferent. To be sure, some are more indifferent than others. Some are not indifferent at all. But where there is indifference it must be challenged. There can be no compromise. Either Jesus is Lord or he isn't. If he is, we stay in. If he isn't, we get out.

In the seventies of the first century people were leaving the church right and left. It was the best thing that ever happened to it. In the face of the appalling crisis of their times, those who could not stay with Jesus and risk their lives left Jesus and saved their lives. You could not blame those who left. But we are in churches today because of those who stayed.

The church in 2000 will be lean. It will be stripped. Already the process has begun. Every year the growth in church membership fails to keep pace with the growth of the population. It is the best thing that could happen to the church.

Either Jesus is Lord or he isn't. If he is, he makes demands. "You are my friends *if* you do what I command you." Love your neighbor. Love your enemy. Feed the starving. Clothe the naked. Form the Third Force to do something about the gut issues in your community. If the demands are not for us, then we are not for the church. The church in 2000 will be stripped of all the people who could not meet the demands. They will fall away just as they did in the first seventies and eighties and nineties.

II

Two, there will be no denominations. There were none in the first church and there will be none in the twenty-first-century church. It is just too much baggage to carry. You can't be lean and carry all that denominational weight. By the same token, a divided church just simply cannot meet the agony of its time.

How this will happen is anybody's guess. But the pressure is on and will not let up. The smaller the church becomes, the less it needs its ossified structures. We are going two ways trying to shed our denominational skins. On the one hand, there is the Consultation on Church Union which wants to bring us all together under one tent. On the other hand, there are local coalitions seeking to split us up into many tents. They are composed of Catholics and Protestants and men of good will everywhere who see the agony and want to meet it.

The coalition people have little time for the Consultation people. The structure at the top, they say, is not as important as the structure at the bottom. While hierarchs debate what to call the clergy in the new church, the "lower archs" put together small groups of people who will risk their money and time to help those who are persecuted in their own community and elsewhere.

Just two blocks from where Lenin held his revolutionary strategy sessions, met the leaders of the Orthodox Church. And of all the urgent topics that might have been considered . . . these prelates held lengthy discussions on the color, cut and style of church vestments.[1]

III

Three, there will be no buildings. There were none in the first century except the one that brought all the trouble, namely, the temple in Jerusalem. The reason they went after Stephen and the reason they went after Jesus was that both of them said the temple was secondary rather than primary.

Today the building is once again primary, a fact which is simply and precisely reflected by the budget of nearly every church in the nation. The most important man in the church is the janitor. Next is the chairman of the finance committee, who is desperately trying to pay off the mortgage. Next is the wealthiest member of the congregation who pays most of it.

There were no buildings in the seventies or eighties or nineties of the first century, or in the second century. The first Christians worshiped where they lived. They worshiped in their homes. They had what were called "house churches." They most certainly did not have all their money tied up in some church "plant" somewhere, making it impossible for them to move to do something about the agonies of their time.

In 2000 there will be nothing more permanent than tents. All the old buildings will either be in disrepair or will have been given to the community in which they were built as a symbol of the servanthood on which the church was founded. The church meanwhile will be worshiping in the homes of its trimmed-down membership.

Again the handwriting is on the wall. The construction of religious buildings in America dropped off 7 percent in 1968, to just under $1.1 billion—which, incidentally, is a whopping sum in itself.[2] In 1969 it was down to $949 million.[3]

IV

Four, there will be no Sunday School. There was none in the first century and there is no reason why there should be one in the twenty-first. As a matter of fact, there is only one reason there ever was a Sunday School in the first place. It was introduced in nineteenth-century America to educate children who had no parents. There is not now and there never has been any reason why there should be a substitute—as opposed to supplementary—Sunday School for children who have parents who vowed in their baptismal vows to "bring up their children in the nurture and admonition of the Lord." Either they will or they won't. If they will, they stay in the church. If they won't by 2000 they will be gone from the church.

Where did we ever get the idea that educating *our* children in *our* religion was the responsibility of some *other* mother or father? Talk about indifference! How could we be much more indifferent than refusing to teach our own children the most important thing we will ever have to teach them?

There are ways to do this. They are being used. The main thing is to equip the *parents*. After all, Jesus blessed the children and taught the adults.

Some years ago, Hartshorne and May made a study of the moral attitudes of children compared with the various other significant persons in their lives. They found the following correlations:

Parent and child .55
Friends and child .35
School teacher and child .03
Sunday School Teacher and child .002.[4]

As a corollary, of course, the need for a building is less when the need for a substitute Sunday School is nil.

V

Five, by 2000 Sunday worship as we know it will be no more. Since there will be no buildings, the form of the worship will have to change. Or, it could be argued, because the form of worship *is* changing that is another reason why there will be no buildings.

There was no set form of worship in the first-century church. There were only the basics. The basics were people, prayer, scripture, discussion, bread, wine. Now the bread and the wine are six times a year or "once a month," which has, of course, nothing whatever to do with first-century worship. We do not know, but it is entirely possible that the church in Laodicea had gotten away from weekly Communion. They had certainly gotten away from worship that made any difference.

You are neither cold nor hot. Would that you were cold or hot! (Rev. 3:15)

As to the other basics, the people in 2000 will at last be loosened up to the point where the spirit can get through. Now everybody worships on his own island in his best clothes in an immaculate building. That may be one form of worship, but it is not the only form. Indifference, lukewarmness—as with teaching our own children, as with putting too much money in our buildings, as with letting our membership grow fat rather than lean—have led us on too many occasions to freeze out the spirit. People are not touched. The word is not encountered. Silence is not shared.

But experiments are beginning. They will not stop. Attendance at worship is at its lowest since the Gallup Poll began polling attendance at worship. It is a good sign. It means that people are fed up with forms that are calcified. And it means that, by 2000, form will follow function and what we do on Sunday will be as natural to what we do on Monday as leaves are to a tree. It may, of course, not even be done on Sunday at all.

VI

Six, the church in 2000 will be full of people taking risks for love. This is not to say there are not such people in churches now. It is only to say that by 2000 *only* such people will be left in churches. Like the man who risked his life to write what he wrote to the church in Laodicea.

The opposite of love is not hate but indifference. The sin of the Laodicean church was not that they hated Jesus. It was not that they hated Domitian. It was that they were indifferent to both. They would not risk for either. And they would not risk for each other.

James Forman went to the churches last year and said, We need your help. He was trying to put something together for black people. And what was the churches' reaction? Some raised money. But the reaction of many was "blackmail," "Communism," and other choice epithets on the lips of Christians. We did not realize that it was our indifference, our lukewarmness, our unwillingness to risk that made James Forman do what he did in the first place—and the Chicago Seven, and Father Groppi, and Dr. King.

The people of the church in 2000 will be warm, not lukewarm. A man said he went home from worship with tears in his eyes. "I could sense the vibrations," another man said, who is doing a Christian thing on the south side of a large city. "People were in community," he said. And then he added, "That's what it's all about."

Church is people being warm with people, not lukewarm. Only the warm people will be left by 2000. Church is a young man home from college with the word "love" on his lips. Church is a young mother telling how it is between her and her friends when they share the deep things of life. Church is the person who said, "You're different when you're involved in other people's sadness." Church is the girl who went away, being hugged when she comes back.

VII

Seven, the church in 2000 will have the Bible back. If the church in Laodicea had read their scrolls it would have been different. But reading the scroll was not their style. Finance and commerce and medicine were. Therefore they could be indifferent to what was going on around them. It doesn't have to be that way, but it was. If you read the Bible, it should never be that way.

We can sit loose to structure, but we cannot sit loose to the Bible. The structure *follows* the Bible. Form follows function. The function of the church is to break open the word as well as to break the bread. *Anything* that allows the word to be broken is permissible.

Already the signs are there. "I have to get more of the Bible." a man said. "I'm hungry for it. I want a course in it, this fall, in this church, as solid as any course I took in college."

The Bible lasts. *Every* institutional form is up for grabs. Only the Bible remains. And *only* the institutional form that allows the Bible to be heard will fit. *Every* form must follow that function.

> Hear, you mountains, the controversy of the Lord,
>   and you enduring foundations of the earth;
> for the Lord has a controversy with his people,
>   and he will contend with Israel.
>
> (Mic. 6:2)

VIII

Eight, the church in 2000 will have a sense of urgency. It will speak, not be silent. It will be passionate, not bloodless. It will be on fire, not lukewarm any more.

That was the word the early Christians used, only it wasn't a metaphor then, it was a fact.

I counsel you [the writer to the Laodiceans wrote for Christ] to buy from me gold refined by fire. (Rev. 3:18)

He was telling all the rich people in the fat church at Laodicea to risk their lives in the martyrs' fires or make a mockery of their faith.

What we need is the moral equivalent of the martyr's fire to galvanize our faith into action and our action into faith. Already there are signs that it is coming. There are people who hurt because there are people who hurt. "We need people," a "Laodicean" said, "with fire in their guts to do what needs to be done." The church in 2000 will be lean and spare and hot enough to do instantly what needs to be done to let the *agape* and the justice for which they once were famous through.

IX

Nine, and then all the young people will come back. They will be in the churches again. Because they have laughed and cried with the warm and beautiful people who risked so much for one another, who pored over a book that they took to their very hearts—people who had this terrible sense of urgency from that book and from each other about the hurt that was in their world, and about how, with the Suffering Servant beside them, healing was in their hands, and the world *could* be turned upside down.

APPENDIX

Appendix

A Church Plan

Principles Observed
1. Simple enough for mother-in-law.
2. Strategic plan kept to one umbrella item only, for simplicity and focus.
3. Increasingly detailed as move from strategy through tactics to operations.
4. Must be written by the church's chief executive officer, namely the minister or priest.

St. Luke Church Plan

   I. *What* we want to be: a suffering servant.
  II. *How* we will become it: we will study, share, serve.
 III. *When* it will be done and *who* will do it: now, everyone.

Strategic Or Overall Plan

I. *What* we want to become: a suffering servant.

  A. Our job is to be what Jesus was, individually and collectively.

  B. It is to show the young, the poor, the black, the dispossessed, that their burden is ours.

  C. It is to challenge the old, the rich, the white, the propertied to take up their cross.

  D. It is in so doing to experience the love, joy, and peace of Christ.

Tactical Or Management Plan

II. *How* we will become it: by studying, sharing, serving.

Every member will study, share, serve Christ.
Every member will think, feel, act Christ.
Every member will use brain, heart, muscle for Christ.

We will form a think tank for Christ.
We will form a family for Christ.
We will form a cadre for Christ.

We will use our intellectual equipment.
We will use our emotional equipment.
We will use our behavioral equipment.

A. We will *study* Christ.
   1. We will read the Bible.
   2. We will look for Christ.
       a. We will find him in our homes.
       b. We will find him in our community.

B. We will *share* Christ.
   1. Personally.
       a. We will divide ourselves into small groups.
       b. We will make our large groups intimate.
       c. We will make our smallest groups, our families, intimate.
       d. We will draw others into our groups.
   2. Impersonally.
       a. We will tithe.
       b. We will give away 51% of our income.

C. We will *serve* Christ.
   1. Through social service.
       a. We will divide ourselves into task forces.
       b. We will treat symptoms.
       c. We will use 40% of our benevolences.
   2. Through social action.

    a. We will divide ourselves into cadres.
    b. We will treat causes.
    c. We will use 60% of our benevolences.
    d. We will organize for social change.
       1. Through companies.
       2. Through political parties.
       3. Through the church.
       4. Through other institutions.

OPERATIONAL PLAN

III *When* it will be done and *who* will do it: now, everyone.
  A. When: 1971
    1. *Study*
      a. By the end of 1971, 50% of the church school will be given the option of the Character Research Curriculum.*
      b. By the end of 1971, 25% of the church school teachers will be men, 25% youth, 10% children, 40% women.
      c. By the end of 1971, 75% of the senior highs will be in the youth group.
      d. By the end of 1971, 33% of the congregation will be studying the Bible.
    2. *Share*
      a. Personal
        1. By the end of 1971, 50% of the congregation will be in small groups.
        2. By the end of 1971, 33% of the families will have learned how to share.
        3. By the end of 1971, at least 9 "Advances" will have been held.**
        4. By the end of 1971, 100% of the college-age members will have had some meaningful contact with the church.
        5. By the end of 1971, 100% of the worship services will be intimate.

  *Published by Union College Character Research Project, 10 Nott Terrace, Schenectady, N.Y. 12308.
  **Retreats.

6. By the end of 1971, the participating membership will have increased by 5%, the non-participating by 0%.
7. By the end of 1971, 100% of the congregation will participate in studying, sharing, serving.

b. Impersonal

1. By the end of 1971, 20% of all pledging units will tithe.
2. By the end of 1971, total pledged income will have increased 20%.
3. During 1971, all who join the church during the year will be asked to pledge to the Annual Fund and the Benevolence Fund.
4. By the end of 1971, arrearages in the Annual Fund and the Benevolence Fund will not exceed 5%.
    i. Any who are more than 2 months behind in their Annual giving will be counseled with by a member of the Stewardship Committee.
    ii. Any who are more than 2 months behind in their Benevolence Fund giving will be counseled with by a member of the Benevolence Committee.
5. By the end of October, 1971, a meaningful stewardship program will have been devised for the following:
    i. Children
    ii. Junior Highs
    iii. Senior Highs
    iv. College-Age
    The possibility of class agents will be explored.
6. By the end of May, 1971, all givers below the average, except in cases of known need, will be counseled with by a member of the Stewardship Committee.
7. By the end of 1971, 51% of income will be spent on benevolences.
8. During 1971, no money will be given away until it is shown, in writing, how it will multiply by attracting other money.
9. During 1971, all benevolence money will be split 40–60 between social service and social action.

    10. During 1971, no money will be given unless the project is experiencing difficulty obtaining funds elsewhere.

    11. By the end of February, 1971, all who have not pledged to the Benevolence Fund will have been asked to do so.

3. *Serve*

  a. Social Service

    1. By the end of 1971, 20% of the congregation will be in task forces.

    2. By the end of 1971, no new task forces will have been launched.

    3. By the end of 1971, 40% of benevolences will have been spent on social service.

  b. Social action

    1. By the end of 1971, 10% of the congregation will be in cadres (social action groups).

    2. By the end of 1971, at least one major social ill will have been attacked.

    3. By the end of 1971, 60% of benevolences will have been spent on social action.

    4. By the end of 1971, the 10% of the congregation in cadres will be divided as follows:

      i. 2% companies

      ii. 2% political parties

      iii. 2% church

      iv. 4% other institutions

B. Who: Everyone, with responsibility for seeing that it is done vested in the following:

1. *Study* (letter corresponds with letter at III.A. 1.*a.*, page 156).

  a. Children's Education Committee

  b. Children's Education Committee

  c. Youth-Adult Education Committee

  d. Youth-Adult Education Committee

2. *Share* (letters and numbers correspond).

  a. Personal

    1. Youth-Adult Committee

    2. Youth-Adult Committee

    3. Youth-Adult Committee

    4. Youth-Adult Committee
    5. Worship Committee
    6. New-Member Committee
    7. Membership Committee
  b. Impersonal
    1. Stewardship Committee
    2. Stewardship Committee
    3. Stewardship Committee
    4. Stewardship Committee
    5. Stewardship Committee
    6. Stewardship Committee
    7. Benevolence Committee
    8. Benevolence Committee
    9. Benevolence Committee
    10. Benevolence Committee
    11. Benevolence Committee
3. *Serve* (letters correspond).
  a. Social Service Committee
  b. Social Action Committee

Notes

CHAPTER 1. A Church That Means Business

1. Protestant church attendance during an average week in 1969 was 37%. *Yearbook of American Churches* (New York: National Council of Churches, 1971), p. 221.
2. Protestant benevolence giving averages 35 cents a week. *Church Financial Statistics and Related Data* 1970 (New York: National Council of Churches, 1970), p. 7.
3. Total church membership increased .03% in 1970, *Yearbook, op. cit.*, p. 186.
4. Halford Luccock, *The Interpreter's Bible* (New York and Nashville: Abingdon, 1951), Vol. 1, p. 804.
5. Dietrich Bonhoeffer, *The Cost of Discipleship* (New York: Macmillan, 1963), p. 72 (ital. add.).
6. *Church Financial Statistics, op. cit.*, p. 6.
7. Dietrich Bonhoeffer, *Life Together* (New York: Harper & Row, 1954), p. 110.
8. *Church Financial Statistics, op. cit.*, pp. 4-6.
9. H. Beyer in G. Kittel, *Theological Dictionary of the New Testament* (Grand Rapids: Eerdmans, 1966), Vol. 2, p. 86.
10. Wilbur Elston, "Social, but Little Action," *Christian Century*, January 24, 1962.

CHAPTER 2. Objections to a Church That Means Business

1. Albert Camus, *Resistance, Rebellion, and Death* (New York: Knopf, 1961), p. 71.

CHAPTER 3. The Church and Social Action

1. *1970 New York Times Almanac*, p. 304.
2. *Ibid.*, p. 301.
3. *Ibid.*, p. 302.
4. *Idem.*
5. Richard Parker, *Center Magazine*, March, 1970.
6. *New York Times* Editorial, April 18, 1971.
7. W. S. Coffin, *Minneapolis Tribune*, April 10, 1970.

8. *Minneapolis Star,* April 9, 1970.
9. Parker, *op. cit.*
10. Milton Rokeach, *Psychology Today,* April, 1970.
11. Dick Gregory, *Nigger: An Autobiography* (New York: Dutton, 1964) pp. 216–217.

CHAPTER 4. Objections to the Church and Social Action

1. Quoted in *Monday Morning,* February, 9, 1970.
2. *Trans-Action,* July, 1968.
3. Bernard Berelson and Gary Steiner, *Human Behavior—An Inventory of Scientific Findings* (New York: Harcourt, Brace & World, 1964), p. 576.
4. E. R. Achtemeier, *The Interpreter's Dictionary of the Bible* (New York and Nashville: Abingdon, 1962), Vol. 4, p. 81.
5. Quoted in *Presbyterian Life,* March 1, 1963 (ital. add.)
6. Quoted in *Christianity and Crisis,* October 30, 1967.
7. Quoted in *New York Times,* December 1, 1964.

CHAPTER 5 The Church and Justice

1. E. R. Achtemeier, *The Interpreter's Dictionary of the Bible* (New York and Nashville: Abingdon, 1962), Vol. 4, p. 80.
2. *Ibid.,* p. 81.
3. P. J. Achtemeier, *The Interpreter's Dictionary of the Bible* (New York and Nashville: Abingdon, 1962), Vol. 4, p. 99.
4. E. R. Achtemeier, *op. cit.,* p. 81 (ital. add.).
5. *Christian Century,* November 30, 1966.
6. *New Republic,* April 15, 1970.
7. *Saturday Review,* February 11, 1967.
8. *Minneapolis Tribune,* April 19, 1970.
9. James Madison, *Federalist 10* (ital. add.).
10. *Presbyterian Life,* November 1, 1967, p. 14.
11. John Gardner, quoted by James Reston, *Minneapolis Tribune,* June 25, 1970 (ital. add.).
12. *The Philadelphia Inquirer,* December 23, 1968.

CHAPTER 6. The Church as a Third Force in America

1. R. B. Y. Scott, *The Relevance of the Prophets* (New York: Macmillan, 1959), p. 167.
2. *Ibid.,* p. 177 (ital. add.).

CHAPTER 7. The Marks of a Successful Church

1. *U.S. News and World Report,* June 16, 1969.
2. Alfred Balk, *The Religion Business* (Richmond, Va.: John Knox, 1968), p. 7.
3. *Idem.*

4. *Church Financial Statistics and Related Data* 1970 (New York: National Council of Churches, 1970), p. 6.
5. *U.S. News and World Report*, June 1, 1970.
6. Quoted in Minnesota Synod Lutheran, January, 1966.
7. T. S. Eliot, "The Family Reunion," in *The Complete Poems and Plays* (New York: Harcourt Brace Jovanovich, 1952), p. 281. Reprinted with permission of Harcourt Brace Jovanovich and of Faber and Faber, London.

CHAPTER 8. The Church in Business

1. Sidney Lens, *The Military-Industrial Complex* (Philadelphia: Pilgrim Press, 1970), p. 4.
2. *Ibid.*, p. 12.
3. *Ibid.*, p. 7.
4. *Ibid.*, p. 8.
5. *Idem.*
6. *Ibid.*, p. 22.
7. Judd Polk in *Saturday Review*, November 22, 1969.
8. Lens, *op. cit.*, p. 29.
9. Andrew Hacker, *New York Times Magazine*, July 3, 1966.
10. ———, *New York Times Magazine*, November 12, 1967.
11. T. J. Watson, Jr., *A Business and Its Beliefs* (New York: McGraw-Hill, 1963), p. 77 (ital. add.).
12. Raymon H. Mulford, *Saturday Review*, January 13, 1968 (ital. add.).
13. Hazel Henderson, *Harvard Business Review*, July and August, 1968.
14. Andrew Hacker, *New York Times Magazine*, July 3, 1966.
15. Sol Linowitz, quoted in *Minneapolis Tribune*, May 15, 1970 (ital. add.).
16. Peter Drucker, quoted in *Think* (IBM), November and December, 1965.

CHAPTER 10. The Church and Money

1. All church financial statistics from *Church Financial Statistics and Related Data* 1970 (New York: National Council of Churches, 1970).
2. *Statistics of Church Finances, 1966* (New York: National Council of Churches, 1966), p. 1. This is the latest year for which foreign mission figures are available.
3. Sylvia Porter, *Minneapolis Tribune*, October 31, 1965.
4. Babson Institute *Newsletter*, July 5, 1965.
5. *New York Times*, November 7, 1965.

CHAPTER 11. The Church and Peace Within

1. H. Greeven in G. Kittel, *Theological Dictionary of the New Testament* (Grand Rapids, Mich.: Eerdmans, 1966), Vol. 2, p. 792.
2. *Ibid.*, p. 805.
3. *Ibid.*, p. 804.

4. Sherman E. Johnson in *The Interpreter's Bible* (New York and Nashville: Abingdon, 1952), Vol. 7, p. 308.
5. C. W. F. Smith in *The Interpreter's Dictionary of the Bible* (New York and Nashville: Abingdon, 1962), Vol. 3, p. 867.
6. *Ibid.*, p. 867.
7. Alfred North Whitehead, *Religion in the Making* (New York: Macmillan, 1926), p. 18.
8. Smith, *op. cit.*, p. 862.
9. *Ibid.*, p. 855.
10. Greeven, *op. cit.*, p. 803 (ital. add.).

CHAPTER 13. The Church as Slave

1. W. Foerster in G. Kittel, *Theological Dictionary of the New Testament* (Grand Rapids, Mich.: Eerdmans, 1965), Vol. 3, p. 1086.

CHAPTER 14. The Church as Servant

1. President John Bennett, quoted in *Dubuque Report*, Fall, 1968.
2. *Faith at Work*, December, 1962, p. 23.
3. From *At Ease*, quoted in *New York Times Book Review,* June 18, 1967.
4. R. R. Wicks, *The Interpreter's Bible* (New York and Nashville: Abingdon, 1952) Vol. 11, p. 54.
5. *New York Times*, May 1, 1966.
6. Quoted from *The Kingdom of God in America*, in *Christian Century*, June 15, 1960.
7. Ethelbert Stauffer in Kittel, *Theological Dictionary* (Grand Rapids, Mich.: Eerdmans, 1964), Vol. 1, p. 48 (ital. add.).

CHAPTER 15. The Church is a Sleeping Giant

1. Maya Pines, "You Can Raise Your Child's IQ," *Reader's Digest*, December, 1968.
2. ———, "Why Some 3-Year-Olds Get A's," *New York Times Magazine*, July 6, 1969.
3. ———, "You Can Raise Your Child's IQ."
4. Edward de Bono, "The Virtues of Zigzag Thinking," *Think* (IBM), May-June, 1969.
5. *Time*, October 11, 1963.
6. *Idem.*
7. Halford Luccock, *The Interpreter's Bible* (New York and Nashville: Abingdon, 1952), Vol. 7, p. 809.
8. Tertullian, quoted in Elton Trueblood, *The Company of the Committed* (New York: Harper & Row, 1961), p. 101.
9. John Gardner, "How to Prevent Organizational Dry Rot," *Harper's Magazine*, October, 1965.
10. Dietrich Bonhoeffer, *Life Together* (New York: Harper & Row, 1954), p. 97.

11. *Idem.*
12. *Ibid.,* p. 99.
13. *Idem.*
14. *Ibid.,* p. 101.
15. *Ibid.,* p. 102.
16. Alfred Balk, *loc. cit.* and "America's Churches: Billion Dollar Businesses," *This Week,* June 22, 1969.
17. *Idem.*
18. John T. Garrity, *Harvard Business Review,* June, 1968.
19. 1967 Report of the Minneapolis City Council's Commission on Human Development.

CHAPTER 16. What's Right with the Church

1. Adrian Boufard, quoted in *Time Magazine,* December 25, 1964.
2. *Monday Morning,* October 24, 1960.
3. Quoted in *Time,* January 25, 1967.

CHAPTER 17. The Church in 2000

1. David Poling, *This Week,* May 11, 1969.
2. *Christian Century,* February 26, 1969.
3. *Statistical Abstract of the United States* (Washington, D.C.: U.S. Bureau of the Census, 1970), p. 670.
4. Wallace Denton, *What's Happening to Our Families?* (Philadelphia: Westminster, 1963), p. 120.

72 73 10 9 8 7 6 5 4 3